GÖRAN THERBORN was born in 1941 in Kalmar, Sweden. He has published numerous writings on social theory and class struggle in Swedish, including *Classes and Economic Systems* (1971) and *What is the Value of Good Values?* (1973). He has been an editor of the Scandinavian socialist journal *Zenit*, and is a frequent contributor to *New Left Review* and *Marxism Today* in England. His major essay on the Frankfurt School is included in *Western Marxism — A Critical Reader* (Verso 1983). In 1976 he published the fundamental comparative work on classical sociology and historical materialism, *Science, Class and Society* (Verso 1980). In 1985 he was a Simon Schiot Research Fellow at the University of Manchester. Göran Therborn has taught in the USA, Australia, France, Mexico and Sweden and currently teaches political science at the University of Nijmegen, Netherlands.

Also available from Verso:

What Does the Ruling Class Do When
   it Rules?   £5.95
The Ideology of Power and the
   Power of Ideology   £3.95

Göran Therborn

Göran Therborn

Why Some Peoples are More Unemployed Than Others

VERSO

The Imprint of New Left Books

British Library
Cataloguing in Publication Data

Therborn, Göran
    Why some peoples are more unemployed than
    others: the strange paradox of growth
    and unemployment.
    1. Unemployment 2. Economic development
    I. Title
    331.13'79177   HD5707.5

First published 1986
© Göran Therborn 1986

Verso
15 Greek Street, London W1V 5LF

Typeset in Times Roman by
Leaper & Gard Ltd., Bristol

Printed by The Thetford Press
Thetford, Norfolk

ISBN 0-86091-109-8
ISBN 0-86091-817-3 Pbk

CONTENTS

Preface

Unemployment has become the plague of advanced capitalism in the 1980s. To approach it from a comparative perspective comes naturally for a Swede transplanted to the Netherlands, where the German and British experiences are close at hand. The Netherlands and Sweden are both very developed countries, with the world's highest levels of welfare provision. Yet one is a country of mass unemployment — in 1984 14 per cent of the labour force in the Netherlands were without work — while the other has maintained an unemployment rate below 3.5 per cent throughout the crisis. Similarly, it is not surprising that West Germany should have lower unemployment than Britain. But why the rate of *employment* — the percentage of the adult population in paid work — should be lower in the vigorous and supposedly hard-working Federal Republic than in Britain, and why labour market participation in West Germany, alone among advanced capitalist countries, should have declined since 1965 provides much food for thought.

European experiences, it need hardly be said, have long ceased to be synonymous with the development of advanced capitalism. Visits to and friendships in Australia, Canada, Japan and the USA have taught me much (not necessarily enough) about the New World of advanced capitalism, and the impressive statistical output of the OECD makes these countries amenable to study from afar.

My concern with unemployment is both political — as an intellectual attached to the labour movement — and scientific. The political aspect will not be expressed in denunciations and exhort-

9

ations, however, but in the offering of a set of scientifically grounded political options and experiences to all those who are concerned with unemployment. Besides being empirical and comparative, my approach to the problem is historical and materialist. This is not because I try to hammer home 'the fundamental concepts of historical materialism', or to prove the century-old theses of Karl Marx. My approach is historical in the sense of relating present-day unemployment to the history of the contemporary capitalist crisis; and it is materialistic in that it focuses on material means and constraints that lie beneath the lofty realm of political rhetoric and economic doctrine.

Like all ambitious authors, I would claim that this book puts forward something novel. If that had not been the case I would not have bothered to write it. However, like all serious writers I can only say that I rest on the shoulders of others.

A pioneer of large-scale comparative explanation of differentials in unemployment among nations in the current period has been Manfred Schmidt, now at the Free University of Berlin.[1] My major disagreements with Schmidt are two-fold: one methodological, and one conceptual. Methodologically, I argue that an adequate explanation has to start from an analysis of policy orientations that is situated in a historical and a socio-economic context. While paying increasing attention to policy, Schmidt still tends to search for institutional patterns which regulate the economy and class conflicts. In my view, this results in a certain historical insensitivity.[2]

The other disagreement relates to Schmidt's enduring attachment to the corporatist problematic. He holds that there are two roads to full employment, one 'corporatist and welfare statist' most clearly represented by Sweden and Norway, with Japan constituting a sub-variant of 'corporatism without labour' and one of 'national-liberal-social partnership' represented by Switzerland.

There are also two roads to mass unemployment, one 'pluralist-sectoralist', taken by all the high unemployment countries except the 'pluralist' ones: Australia, Canada and the USA. The key concepts here are not made very clear. Tripartite coordination across policy areas, a criterion distinguishing corporatist from pluralist-sectoralist countries has, in fact, been much more developed in 'pluralist-sectoralist' Finland than in 'corporatist' Sweden or Norway. It is clearly more developed in Belgium than in those two countries, and still more extensive, and by far more institutionalized in the Netherlands.[3] And to call Japan, with its capital-labour relations fragmented among enterprises, more corporatist than the three 'pluralist-sectoralist' countries just mentioned hardly makes much sense either. Nevertheless, by careful empirical investigation of variations in macroeconomic performance and by searching for their determinants, Schmidt has made a major contribution to comparative political economy. To me, Manfred Schmidt has become not only an inspiring colleague, but also a precious friend. I want to thank him particularly for a most pleasant early summer evening in Berlin, which ended with us carrying out joint statistical work.

Another important approach has been developed by Fritz Scharpf at the Science Centre in West Berlin. He was, until August 1984, head of its Labour Market Policy unit, which under Scharpf's directorship developed into the world's leading labour-market research centre. An invitation to the Science Centre in Berlin, for which I am indebted to Peter Tergeist and Frieder Naschold, brought me into direct contact with the impressive West German–West Berlin research on comparative labour-market policy and the politics of work. Scharpf has criticized the explanations of economic performance deriving from the corporatist problematic of Schmitter and Lehmbruch for the insufficient attention they pay to economic constraints and for their too narrow conceptions of institutional structures and of relevant economic indicators. His own analysis has centred on congruent and incongruent policies under institutional constraints, fiscal, monetary, and labour market policy. His comparative work has focused primarily (though not exclusively) on Austria, Sweden and West Germany.[4]

The limitations of his work are mainly its restricted comparative range and the insufficient attention paid to socio-political history. Its strength is the author's firm grasp of economic policy options and implications.

At the Trade Union Movement Centre for Research and Documentation in Oslo, Jon Eivind Kolberg and associates are also developing an extensive, carefully researched critique of standard economic explanations of unemployment, but to this writer's knowledge, they have not so far offered an explanation of their own.[5] A very valuable, non-technical discussion of the main economic constraints of policies for full employment is provided by the British economic historian Derek Aldcroft,[6] although from a comparative point of view it suffers from a focus mainly restricted to the British Isles.

Important new studies or data are almost certain to turn up after a study of this sort is completed. In this case, I came across Michael Bruno's and Jeffrey Sachs's major work, *The Economics of Worldwide Stagflation*,[7] too late to take account of its findings. Though not primarily concerned with the same questions as this book, their technically very sophisticated economic analysis of the post-1973 crisis is certainly highly pertinent to it. There are two main points of agreement between their conclusions and mine. One is that the sharp rise in unemployment (in most countries) was mainly due to restrictive economic policies, with Bruno and Sachs here stressing monetary policy. The second is that national institutions are crucial to the different functioning of economies and should be taken into account by macroeconomic analysts. The disagreements which seem implied in the two very differently analytical approaches relate to their allocating a much greater role to wage developments and wage-determining institutions to the neglect, in my view, of overall politico-economic institutions. Rigid high wages have certainly contributed to unemployment in some countries, but the evidence does not sustain the thesis that labour-cost developments have caused the current divide between the low unemployment countries and the seemingly permanent mass unemployment in most of the Western world.

While policy-making is left out by Bruno and Sachs, albeit appearing to have decisive effects, it is the topic of Paul Mosley's *The Making of Economic Policy*,[8] which is a very penetrating comparative study of the UK and the USA since 1945. Its pluralist political perspective of governments and voters would no doubt have changed if the author had included a full employment country, from which vantage-point the fruitfulness of a more elaborate historical institutional approach would have emerged more clearly. I have also benefited greatly from the critical comments of Andrew Glyn, Gunnar Olofsson and Gunnar Persson. Their questioning has posed some very important challenges.

I would particularly like to thank Huub Spoormans, Jacques Sauren, Joop Roebroek, Arend Geul and Roel in't Veld for having widened my vision by bringing me to the Netherlands. The empirical spadework for this book has not been done by anonymous research assistants, humbly contributing to the career of their professor, and I have to claim sole responsibility for whatever misjudgements and miscalculations may have been reached. But two students of mine, Rien Wijnhoven and Wessel Visser, have been very stimulating collaborators in this endeavour, and their specific contributions are indicated below. My methodological colleague, Ton Bertrand, saved me considerable time by offering the resources of his computer programming skills.

A rough, first version of this study was written for a conference on the contemporary crisis, organized by the Faculties of Economics and Politics of the UNAM and the Metropolitan University of Mexico. The reception it received there, and the conference discussion, were an important stimulus to continue the work. Thanks to the kindness of Elmar Altvater and Michael Dauderstädt, I also had the opportunity to test some of the ideas in this book at a Friedrich-Ebert-Stiftung conference held in Bonn in September 1984.

Without the enormous statistical and other investigative work by the OECD Secretariat and its mainly anonymous researchers, this kind of study would not have been possible. Thanks are also due to the statisticians of the European Community, the US Bureau of Labor Statistics, the United Nations Economic Commissions, and the ILO. Finally, I am obliged to Chris Bertram, who had the tough job of editing the various versions of the manuscript.

Nijmegen, June 1984–January 1985
Manchester, April–May 1985
West Berlin, June 1985

Summary and Conclusions

At the end of 1984 there were between thirty-one and thirty-two million unemployed in the OECD heartlands of the capitalist world — a figure representing some 8.2 per cent of the labour force.[1] 1984 was a peak year in a prolonged period of crisis, and in the coming years unemployment is likely to rise even further. The OECD predicts thirty-two million unemployed by mid-1986, of which 20.25 million will be in Europe.[2] A European report co-ordinated by *The Economist* forecasts an unemployment rate of 11.5 per cent in 1989-90 for Belgium, France, West Germany, Italy, Netherlands, and the UK, as compared to 10.5 per cent in 1983-84; the rate will range, in 1990, from 8.2 per cent in Germany to 23.1 per cent in Belgium.[3] A study for the European Community, carried out by the Netherlands Economic Institute in Rotterdam, has projected an unemployment rate for 1990 in the present ten members of the EEC at 12.1 per cent, with an optimistic variant based on high growth rates of 9.4 per cent and a low-growth variant of 18.0 per cent.[4]

In late December 1984 a decorated American Second World War veteran was freezing to death, homeless, a stone's throw from the White House; in Socialist governed France, dire poverty had to be alleviated by charitable food parcels; and in the capital of Denmark — once in the vanguard of welfare-state development, now a country of mass unemployment — young unemployed were queuing, heads bowed in shame, for morning bread and coffee and for food too stale to be sold, which is handed out by the Salvation

14

Army.[5] The misery of the decay of the old industrial inner cities of Britain is already reaching proportions similar to those of the richest country of the capitalist world, the latter's desperate violence, however, has yet to develop in Britain.

In this context, the normal rules of scientific discourse start to lose their significance. We are not just dealing with the scientific problem of explaining mass unemployment, but also with a human problem, with human suffering and frustration. By 1983, there were already about 7.2 million people in OECD Europe who had been unemployed for more than one year.[6] On the other hand, this is not a denunciatory pamphlet, nor a manifesto of political action, it is a work of scientific analysis, by a professional social scientist, using all the basic tools of comparative social science, with many statistical tabulations of data from sixteen different countries, using correlation and regression techniques, and probing into various kinds of economic and labour market policies, and institutions of political economy. There are political and trade union leaders and progressive ideologists much better equipped for polemic and agitation than this writer is.

The conclusions of this study are the outcome of a long and laborious process of research. But, as Marx taught us long ago, the form of presentation need not follow that of research. This book was written for two publics. First, for everybody concerned with the problems of unemployment, in particular trade union and progressive political activists, leaders and journalists; second, for my fellow social scientists throughout the world, regardless of their political stance or concerns. The long odyssey through statistical records and into comparative policy measures is mainly aimed at the latter (many general readers will also no doubt use those parts as sources of reference). The fairly simply statistical techniques used are explained to the lay reader, no special training is required to be able to follow the line of argument. The conclusions, however, are first of all directed to the general reader, to the forces which make history, rather than to those who only explain it. Therefore, the conclusions are presented before the evidence and the line of argument, with a view to making them as easily access-ible as possible. But my cards are on the table. All the evidence is available for inspection and challenge in the three main parts of the book.

This is a study of the causes of unemployment in sixteen countries in the first decade (1974-84) of the current international crisis. The countries are: Australia, Austria, Belgium, Canada, Denmark, Finland, France, Germany, Italy, Japan, the Netherlands, Norway, Sweden, Switzerland, the UK and the USA. The choice is not arbitrary. It covers all the most advanced capitalist countries for which standardized unemployment rates are available, thanks to the efforts of the anonymous statisticians of the OECD. Denmark and Switzerland are also covered, since both unquestionably belong to the cream of contemporary capitalism, and they are countries for which national data are of sufficient reliability and precision to place them on a ranking of unemployment.[7] The study presented here is not an attempt at crisis theory and analysis, the crisis is taken as given. Our concern is to explain the different and diverging effects of the crisis upon unemployment and employment.

This first decade of the crisis has seen a *historic turn* in advanced capitalism. That turn is not simply a rise of mass unemployment, it is a *divergence* in the unemployment rates of different countries. The same international crisis had led to the emergence of a group of mass unemployment countries — Belgium, the Netherlands, Britain, Canada, Denmark — all having a rate of unemployment above ten per cent in 1982, 1983, 1984, and (with the possible exception of Denmark) most likely to keep it there in 1985, 1986 and probably, unless policies change radically, at least for the rest of the decade. Other countries may soon join this club of disaster, Italy did so in the course of 1984, and France in the first month of 1985. A second group is characterized by medium high unemployment (between five and ten per cent). In 1982-84 this group consisted of Italy (1982-83), Australia, the USA, France, Germany, and Finland. Only Finland seems to have a real prospect of regaining full employment in the coming years. Finally, five countries have managed to maintain a rate of unemployment below five per cent: Austria, Sweden, Norway, Japan and Switzerland. They are likely to stay below that ceiling in the future.

Mass unemployment, then is *no fatality*. It is not, as the Dutch Christian Democratic Minister of Social Affairs and Employment, de Koning, has said, 'an anonymous evil force at work, against which we can do nothing.'[8] The same crisis has caused much more unemployment in some countries than in others. The evil forces at work in the mass unemployment countries cannot be attributed to the anonymous world market. Those forces have a name and sometimes also a face. Mr de Koning should be able to recognize many of them in the present Dutch Cabinet.

The divergence of records of unemployment and of efforts to combat it also indicates the poor scholarship and the disgusting cynicism — or should we call it happy ignorance of the lives of the unemployed — of Richardson and Henning in the conclusion to their quite informative book: *Unemployment*:[9] 'For the period 1945-75, Western societies greatly valued full employment as a strategic and overriding political goal. In the decade 1975-85 they may gradually have abandoned that goal, by sheer force of circumstances ... If this transition is taking (or indeed has taken) place, then Western democracies will have demonstrated tremendous strength and maturity in the face of an ever-changing and in some respects unmanageable world.'

My work is aimed at explaining the historical divergences that have appeared in experiences of unemployment during the present crisis. The first part is mainly critical, and gives rise to four main conclusions apart from the differential impact of the crisis on unemployment. Firstly, differences in overall economic growth *and* labour supply can account for only a small part of the differences in levels and increases of unemployment. In fact, they account for only 17 per cent of the variations in unemployment increase between the last pre-crisis peak of the business cycle (in 1973) and the latest peak of the business cycles of the crisis (in 1984). Secondly, crisis exposure and vulnerability, both in terms of world market dependence and economic structure, make only a small contribution to an explanation of why some peoples are more unemployed than others. But it seems to be true that political and cultural independence, while not including economic protectionism or seclusion from the world market, is important. Thirdly, the key tenets of current right-wing liberalism are found to be unsupported by the empirical evidence. There is no significant relationship between inflation and unemployment, none with developments in labour costs, and none with social expenditure and taxation, nor with unemployment compensation.

Fourthly, wage restraint in itself leads neither to full employment nor to successful international competitiveness. Furthermore, there is a zero relationship between labour costs per unit produced in national currency and the same expressed in internationally common currency. In other words, incomes policies can be made as well as unmade by currency policies and changes in the exchange rates. It appears that both left-wing and right-wing economists are wrong in believing, as a universal, non-contextual thesis, that unemployment is dependent on profit rates or on trends of profit rates.

The findings with regard to the welfare state and taxation mean that neither the enemies nor the defenders of the welfare state are generally right. Increases in unemployment are not significantly related to increases and levels of social expenditure and taxation, to the amount of unemployment compensation or to the size of public-sector employment. The relation between the welfare state and full employment has to be re-thought in terms beyond those employed by both its defenders and its attackers.

There is one strong welfare state (Sweden), with generous social commitments, a relatively developed public control of the economy, and an institutionalized commitment to full employment, which has been successful. There are 'soft' welfare states (Belgium, Denmark and the Netherlands) which also have extensive social policies, but have little control of their economies and little concern with and little success against unemployment. A third group of countries are the full-employment-oriented medium welfare states: Austria and Norway. We have also the countries with a mediocre record with respect to social policy and unemployment: Finland, France, Germany, Italy (Britain may be included in terms of social policy, though Thatcherite unemployment policy makes it different in the field of job-loss). Two countries are full employment market states, with very under-developed welfare states: Japan and Switzerland. Finally, there are the market-oriented states *tout court*, all with high unemployment: Australia, Canada and the USA. Finally, as a general conclusion, it emerges that universal market relationships — standard textbook economics and its vulgarly propagated ideologies notwithstanding — explain very little of why the same world-wide crisis has had, and is having, such different effects on unemployment levels.

The second part is descriptive, trying to look more deeply into labour market changes and structures, rather than just looking at the rate of unemployment. Wide differences in the participation in the labour force of youth, women and older males are found, indicating very different locations of work and labour market perspectives in different advanced capitalist societies. The notion of a decline of 'work society' can hardly be sustained. For most of the countries, labour market participation, either as employed or as registered unemployed, has reached a historical peak in the 1980s. Germany is an exception with a declining rate of labour-force participation since 1965. The proportion of the adult population with paid employment differs widely, from about half in the Netherlands to almost four-fifths in Sweden. It is not true that women have been driven out of the labour market in the crisis. Except in Switzerland and Germany, female participation in the labour market has increased substantially. It is older males who are pushed out of the labour markets.

Countries can enter into the post-industrial society by expanding either private or public-sector service employment. The USA leads in the former, Sweden the latter. Actual labour time, by people employed or self-employed on the market, also differs greatly. Two low unemployment countries, Japan and Switzerland, have very long hours, while Sweden has the highest rate of part-time work and the lowest number of actual hours worked by industrial workers.

Unemployment befalls gender and age groups very differently in different countries. In Italy, Belgium, and France, female unemployment is more than twice as high as for males, whereas in the UK unemployment is significantly more frequent among men than among women. Compared to prime-age unemployment, youth unemployment is most severe in Italy, France, Norway, Sweden (before guaranteed part-time employment under the Youth Act), and Finland, and lowest in Germany (Swiss figures are unavailable). Nor has there been any uniform immigration policy in the crisis. Between 1970 and 1980, the proportion of foreign workers grew in Belgium, the Netherlands and Sweden, while it was reduced in Switzerland, Austria and Germany.

On the basis of three dimensions (categories hit, duration of unemployment, and unemployment compensation), a number of *unemployment structures* are identified. For example, there is the *punitive industrial crisis unemployment* in the UK, the *compensated general crisis unemployment* in the Netherlands, the *exclusivist unemployment* (befalling above all women and youth — *punitive* in Italy, *compensated* in Belgium), the *punitive shake-out*, short-term unemployment in the USA, with particular racist features, the *exclusivist adult unemployment* in Germany, and the *compensated marginal unemployment* in the low unemployment countries.

Finally, a set of *labour market profiles* is established, made up by rates of unemployment, of employment (as a percentage of the adult population) and of employment growth in the crisis. Norway was found to have the best employment profile — low unemployment, high employment, and high employment growth — Belgium the worst. Close to the Norwegian situation were Sweden and Japan, close to that of Belgium were the Netherlands and Britain. The USA placed itself in a *mediocrity plus* category, with medium unemployment, medium employment, but with the highest employment growth after Canada in 1973-83. The differential employment growth between Europe and the USA was found to have nothing to do with Reaganomics, as the gap had already appeared in the 1960s. For employed workers, the crisis has been most beneficial, in terms of *real wages*, to Italian, Belgian and French workers, and most disappointing to American, Swedish and British workers. The poor performance of the very strong Swedish trade-union movement is striking.

The third part offers an answer to the basic question of this study; why have some peoples become more unemployed than others? It parts ways with prevailing theses, economic or political, but it would be pretentious to claim that it has no precedents or parallels whatsoever. In the preface I indicated my debt to colleagues. I now offer two main lines of explanation.

Explanation 1: Economic and Political History

The rise of unemployment and the international divergence with regard to unemployment is, first of all, a historical event. An explanation should begin by locating it in time. The current international pattern of unemployment started to emerge only after the onset of the crisis in 1973-74. In the preceding period there had been a converging trend towards full employment. Before the beginning of the crisis, it was Canada, Italy and the USA which had the highest unemployment rates, while today's mass unemployment countries, such as Belgium, the Netherlands and Denmark had full employment. Britain in 1973 also had a lower rate of unemployment than the OECD as a whole.

The post-1973 crisis exhibits two major labour-market trends. One is of continuously rising unemployment, relatively unaffected by cyclical fluctuations. The other is the steadily widening gap between high and low unemployment countries. Along this historical route, we can distinguish two moments of differentiation. One was in 1975, when today's low unemployment countries — Austria, Japan, Norway, Sweden and Switzerland — parted company with the rest, by maintaining an unemployment rate below 2.5 per cent. The next crucial separation took place in 1981-82, when Belgium, Canada, Denmark, the Netherlands and the UK formed a club of their own by plunging into mass unemployment.

There is an economic historical pattern to this process. The differentiation among our sixteen countries took place in the two cyclical troughs of the crisis, which suggest that it is the capacity and the resolve to resist the onslaughts of the international storm, rather than the ability to ride the waves of recovery that have been decisive. This interpretation is further sustained by the cumulative effects of how the depressions were met. The countries which failed in 1974-75, failed even more in 1981-82. The disastrous countries in 1981-82 also failed to benefit from the upturn of 1984. With one partial exception, the countries which maintained full employment in 1975 have managed to do so ever since. Finland was successful in 1975, but has subsequently slipped to a rate of unemployment slightly above six per cent. By early 1985, with unemployment down to 5.1 per cent, Finland was the only high unemployment country with any short-term prospect of returning to more or less full employment.

In policy terms, this kind of historical process strongly indicates, that, contrary to monetarist or supply-side arguments, what matters is not so much anti-inflation or growth policy but employment policy. Variations in economic growth account for less than half of the variation in the growth of unemployment, and the correlation between inflation and unemployment is close to zero.

The differential impact of the same international crisis, and the weakness or virtual absence of significant relationships of economic structure and of general economic process variables to the development of unemployment in the past decade, strongly suggest the relevance of a political explanation. However, the inadequacy of standard political science in the explanation of the recent history of unemployment is hardly less than that of standard economics.

Of the eight countries which joined the historic high unemployment group of Canada, Italy and the USA in the mid-1970s, five had labour (dominated) governments. Of the five successful countries, three had labour and two had bourgeois (dominated) governments. The party character of governments was of little significance. In 1981-82, at the time of division between unemployment failures and disasters, four of the five failure countries had pure bourgeois governments, while one enjoyed a Social Democratic minority cabinet. Among the six high unemployment countries in 1981-82, three had labour-dominated governments. But by then, four out of the five low unemployment states were governed by bourgeois parties.

The more sophisticated and class-oriented classification of the socio-political character of democratic capitalist regimes developed by Walter Korpi is no more helpful here. Korpi has advanced a typology based on rates of unionization (indicator of working-class mobilization) and labour party proportion of cabinet seats (indicator of working-class control).[10] Three of the five low unemployment countries — Austria, Norway, and Sweden — score high on unionization and on labour party postwar cabinet influence, while the two other full employment countries — Japan and Switzerland — score low on both. Among the mass unemployment countries, Belgium and Denmark had, after Sweden, the highest rate of unionization in the capitalist world in 1970-80.[11]

Mainly due to the theoretical background sketched by Manfred Schmidt — who has made a number of important contributions to the comparative study of economic performance — 'corporatism' has come to figure as a possible explanation of variations in unemployment. Definitions and classifications by country of 'corporatism' differ considerably among the advocates of the concept. As a potential explanation of unemployment the subset of definitions and applications of 'corporatism' developed above all by Gerhard Lehmbruch (which focuses on the participation of interest organizations in policy-making) seems most plausible. However, whether one takes structures of 'corporatist concertation' over a broad range of socio-economic policy issues, or if one looks at the frequency of 'corporatist' incomes policies in the 1970s, 'corporatism' turns out to be conducive to low unemployment (Sweden, Austria), medium unemployment (Finland), and to mass unemployment (the Netherlands, Belgium). Corporatist explanations remain therefore unconvincing.

Neither politics in general nor economics in general give us much help here, but our historical overview gives us a clue to what to look for — i.e., something which can account for the differential capacity of countries to resist the tendency of the crisis to raise unemployment. Economic and political structures have turned out to be too crude to do that. An overview of policies alone would be too specific, begging the question of why some policies have been pursued in certain countries and not in others. The solution offered here is to investigate the location of the commitment to full employment in the set-up of national political economic systems. Government responsibility for and concern with (un)employment has everywhere in the postwar period become part of mainstream political discourse. But rhetoric is one thing, institutionalized norms and priorities, backed up by policy-making mechanisms and by internalized expectations of the political and the economic factors are something else.

Analysing the postwar history of our sixteen countries, it was found that in five of them full employment had been firmly institutionalized in the political and economic system before the onslaught of the current crisis. These were Austria, Japan, Norway, Sweden and Switzerland: in other words the only low unemployment countries in the contemporary crisis. *The existence or non-existence of an institutionalized commitment to full employment is the basic explanation for the differential impact of the current crisis.* An institutionalization of the commitment to full employment involves: a) an explicit commitment to maintaining/ achieving full employment; b) the existence and use of countercyclical mechanisms and policies; c) the existence and use of specific mechanisms to adjust supply and demand in the labour market to the goal of full employment; d) a conscious decision not to use high unemployment as a means to secure other policy objectives.

Now, historical explanations are always open to further regression in time. Why was full employment institutionalized as an overriding goal of the national political economy in these five countries and nowhere else? No full and final answer to that question can be offered here. But the immediate causes of the institutionalization and of its reproduction can be clearly identified.

Full employment was institutionalized for two major, quite different reasons. One was an assertion of working-class interests. It owed its success to a politically dominant labour movement, acting against the background of its experiences of the depression of the 1930s, experiences not only of mass unemployment but also of its own capacity in government to alleviate it. Such an attitude might be expected from a Marxist or Kaleckian perspective.[12] But this description fits only Sweden and — with some qualification — Norway, whose labour movements were not only dominant right after the war but were also the only labour movements to both emerge strengthened out of the 1930s — largely because of their anti-unemployment successes, however modest in retrospect — and unscathed by the war.

The second reason for the institutionalization of full employment is more unexpected. It was a conservative concern with order and stability as being of equal importance to capital accumulation. Full employment in Japan and Switzerland has this background. We should be somewhat more precise here. Recent functionalist Marxism has not been blind to bourgeois concerns with order and stability, indeed they have been invoked rather too easily. The point made here is that the post-war Japanese and Swiss bourgeoisies were not at all under threat from the workers' movement (notwithstanding a moment of tension in Japan in 1947), which was weak, divided and largely docile. On the other hand, it cannot be concluded that because the labour movement was so weak or subdued, the Japanese and the Swiss bourgeoisies did not have to bother about maintaining an 'industrial reserve army'. Firstly, because the much weaker American labour movement did not lead to any disappearance of high unemployment nor has the most docile of all labour movements, the Dutch, been rewarded by any stable high employment. Secondly, the Japanese and the Swiss bourgeois class did not simply stop bothering about maintaining an industrial reserve army, they became committed to an active maintenance of full employment (even at high cost, as become evident particularly in Switzerland in the 1970s).

The postwar power blocs in Japan and Switzerland had at least two important things in common. One was a strong pre-capitalist component in a dynamic bourgeois constellation, quasi-feudal in Japan, petit-bourgeois in Switzerland, in both cases bearers of an absolutely central national tradition. A perspective broader than the return on invested capital could therefore be expected from such a ruling bloc. The market had been deified in neither country: it was curtailed by extensive state-backed cartelization in inter-war Switzerland and by monopolization in Japan. The other common feature was that the dominant classes of both countries knew from the 1930s that the impact of a crisis could be significantly mitigated.

Austria falls somewhere in between these two poles, and its

institutionalization of full employment has a different historical foundation. In policy terms, full institutionalization came much later, only in the late sixties and early seventies, while in the other countries it dates back to the forties and early fifties (Japan). The Austrians were lucky in being somewhat out of step with the international business cycle when the crisis broke out, and their early success in averting high unemployment gave a tremendous boost to their self-confidence in standing up to the challenge. Austrian institutionalization was a consequence of working-class self-assertion, conveyed by a Social Democratic party (governing since 1970 and unique in achieving an absolute majority of all votes, in a multi-party system with proportional representation). Order and stability was a common concern of both major parties, who vividly remembered the effects of mass unemployment and civil war in the 1930s — the demise of Austria into Nazi Germany.

The postwar institutionalization of full employment was reproduced and continuously strengthed through its successful re-affirmation. Here the old saying 'nothing breeds success like success' is apt. By this means 'the self-confidence of policy-makers and the expectations of policy-takers' (to use a beautiful expression coined by Claus Offe) were crucially shaped. The primary commitment to achieving and maintaining full employment in the five countries above was neither challenged by other concerns nor by failing performance prior to the major test of the post-1973 crisis. In Britain, by contrast, an institutionalization of full employment, though never clearly formulated either by Beveridge, Keynes or by the 1945 Labour Government, was underway by the late forties, due both to actual labour market outcomes and to the absorption of Keynesian macroeconomics. But the fact that British governments clung to the imperial legacy of the international standing of the pound sterling and the City began to erode this. By the time of the 1966 Labour Government under Harold Wilson, full employment was deliberately sacrificed in the ultimately vain attempts to rescue Britain's financial great power status.

Historical economic policy is the main explanation of the 1974-84 divide between low and high unemployment countries, a divide which, unless met by radical reversals of power and policies, is most likely to set the stage for the 1990s. At the bottom end of the unemployment spectrum, occupied first of all by Belgium, the Netherlands, and the UK, we have seen the application of restrictive monetarism. As in the 1930s, the quickest and surest road to mass unemployment is deflation. In all these countries, failed, divided and demoralized labour movements have given rise to consistently right-wing governments and to new heights of unemployment. In between there are countries with contradictory policies and with policies aggravated or mitigated by particular conditions and tendencies.

However, a true historical and materialist explanation can no more simply repose on the basis of political conditions than it can be satisfied with the correlation and regression exercises of standard comparative social research. We have to show the causal sequences by which the explanatory factors work themselves out in particular contexts.

Explanation 2: Policies under Pressures and Constraints

The causal paths traced in this study have followed labour market as well as macroeconomic policies, under pressures of labour supply developments and under international constraints of trade balances with the rest of the world.

The evidence clearly falsifies the thesis of the OECD 'McCracken Report' of 1977 that 'the road to full employment lies in the recognition of the fact that governments cannot guarantee full employment, independent of the development of prices and wages'.[13] That is, governments can indeed maintain low unemployment in the face of a prolonged crisis, and wages and prices do not on their own have a significant effect upon international variations of unemployment.

With regard to policies, our findings show that countries successful in the sphere of employment have all pursued expansive Keynesian-type policies. The important contribution of the latter to Japanese full employment is particularly striking, much more important than the star performance of the Japanese exporters. But Keynesianism is not enough; a comparative overview of budget policies demonstrates that expansionary, demand-boosting policies were necessary but not sufficient to resist the onslaught of the crisis in the mid-seventies. Not only the successful countries, but also failures, like Germany and Denmark and — though more moderately expansionist — the Netherlands, were reflating their economies then. A policy response that was wide-ranging from the onset appears to have been decisive, at least if followed by a strong, well-timed intervention against later threats (such as in Sweden in 1978-79 and in Japan in 1982) and if provided with a basis of other employment-sustaining policies. The low unemployment countries could, in fact, succeed in the 1981-83 recession in spite of clearly contractive budget policies. Firstly, successful Keynesianism has to be accompanied by consistently complementary monetary policy — in particular a policy of low real interest rates. Second, in all the low unemployment countries, expansive fiscal and monetary policies have been crucially supplemented by nationally specific direct interventions in the market economy.

In the Swedish case, such direct interventions have mainly taken the form of active labour-market policy measures of special public works and public vocational (re)training programmes (at their peak, in 1978-79, such measures reduced unemployment by about four per cent). The extensive vocational training programmes have been rather effective in preparing for jobs on the open market. In 1983, for example, 62 per cent of those had taken such programmes were employed on the open market six months later. A record effectiveness was reached in 1984, with seventy per cent of the trainees employed after six months.[14]

The Norwegians have primarily resorted to massive public subsidies of private employment, a tradition built up even before the coming of North Sea oil and gas revenue. In the late 1970s, this was also a measure amply used in Sweden. Early after the war Norway further set up a sophisticated apparatus of macro-economic planning geared to the maintenance of full employment. After Sweden, Norway was also a pioneer in establishing a unified administration for labour policies, the Labour Directorate, but training and public works programmes in Norway are not at all of the same extent as they have been in Sweden since the 1960s.

The Japanese have relied on expanding public investment, which provides a much higher proportion of total investment than in most capitalist countries, and on a publicly co-ordinated private labour market policy, organized by the big concerns. Behind the sustained growth and exports of Japan in the crisis lies a massive restructuring of Japanese industry, first from textiles, then from shipbuilding and steel, into car-making, electrical engineering, electronics, and services. This has largely taken place without first making people unemployed, typically through intra-firm mobility. Big industrial concerns also opened up service sector activities in order to keep up employment. Maintaining employment in the big companies has not been bought at the cost of unemployment among the subcontractors and other sectors of small business.

Austro-Keynesianism, as the Austrians proudly call their policy pattern, has mainly focused on maintaining investment (directly, this means the large slice of public and public enterprise investment; indirectly it refers to cheap credit for private investment) channelled through a public banking system and specific investment incentives via taxation changes. The claim often heard, both from protagonists and from detractors of the Austrian model, about labour hoarding in public industry is not sustained by comparative evidence about the ratio between the development of production and employment in manufacturing. Little heard of but very important, on the other hand, has been a very restrictive immigration policy, significantly reducing the number of foreign workers during the crisis. Immigrant workers in Austria have fewer labour-market rights than in almost any other advanced capitalist country apart from Switzerland. A tight incomes policy, the necessity of which has been reinforced by the chosen 'hard currency option' of tying the Austrian schilling to the German mark, has also characterized the Austrian model.

Switzerland met the crisis by a massive repatriation of foreign workers, and by an official policy, propagated by the employers' organizations, of laying off women and of discouraging them from entering the labour market. These harsh policies should not, however, be interpreted as simply passing on the costs of the full employment of Swiss males to women and Italian immigrants. The Swiss economy had a record unique within the OECD of zero growth for the 1975-83 period. This probably has also a great deal to do with the singularly weak dose of Keynesian-type expansion policies and with the fact that Switzerland is the only low unemployment country which has pursued a monetarist policy (in the technical sense of setting policy targets for the money supply).

To conclude this section, the state in the low unemployment countries has significant control of one or more strategic economic variables on the market itself, a control which has been amply used to ensure full employment. This has meant control of labour supply in Switzerland and Austria; of labour demand and of qualitative labour supply in Sweden; investment in Japan, Austria and Norway; and price and cost structures in Norway and Austria.

The general argument for and against Keynesianism has often been conducted in mistaken terms. The most effective expansive policies have been directed not so much towards stimulating consumer demand as directly towards investment. Secondly, the effectiveness of fiscal expansion crucially depends on whether or not it is supported by an expansive monetary policy, mainly of low real interest rates and, in some but not all cases, by a deliberate cheap currency policy. Thirdly, successful Keynesianism has, in the current crisis, always been accompanied and reinforced by selective state intervention, and sometimes also by private business not following the dictates of short-term market rationality.

Labour-market pressure upon employment, in the form of labour-supply growth has been more intense in the low unemployment countries than in OECD Europe as a whole, though less severe than in North America. Switzerland is an exception, but Austria is not in spite of its similar pursuit of a policy hostile to foreign workers.

International constraints and the need to adapt to them have had to be faced by the low unemployment countries as well as by the others. But is is probably no accident that these five have — after the USA, and together with Finland — economies that are the least integrated with and least dependent upon the rest of Western capitalism. None is a member of the European Community, and none has its economy deeply penetrated by foreign enterprise. Neither Austrian and Swiss immigration policies, nor Norwegian subsidies, nor the Swedish competitive devaluation of 1982 would have been allowed in the EEC.

The adaptations to international constraints have mainly been successful in the low unemployment countries for two reasons. One is a, not always spectacular but nevertheless general, dynamism and strength of their capitalist economies, in crucial areas (public sector in Austria, private in the others). The case most often noticed is Japanese export performance, but one of the most remarkable examples is the restructuring of the Swiss textile industry into a highly specialized, high-wages export success, and of Swiss export industry at large, which has vigorously expanded, in spite of soaring costs due to the enormous appreciation of the franc. Norway has of course benefited from her North Sea sources of wealth, and Volvo, Electrolux and the other Swedish multinationals have clearly disproved the thesis that dynamic capitalist enterprise is incompatible with strong unions, high taxes, extensive social security, and full employment. On the other hand, this dynamism and strength are neither unique to these countries, nor are they characteristic of these economies as a whole. In fact, all of them have faced serious crises: the Swiss watch industry; Japanese and Swedish shipbuilding; Japanese textiles; Japanese, Swedish, and Austrian steel; and more or less the whole of Norwegian shipping and manufacturing due to oil revenue induced inflation. Also important has further been the self-fulfilling tendency of deeply institutionalized policy orientations. These lead economic factors — business, labour, consumers — to expect that the public orientation of the economy will remain stable and that policy changes are only adaptations to adverse circumstances with long-term goals remaining constant (rather than part of an unpredictable or cyclical stop-go pattern). This stability of expectations makes relative maintenance of employment and investment under worsening conditions, wage moderation by trade unions, stable demand by consumers, and acceptance of low interest rates by financial capital (important in Switzerland), rational options.

The policy analysis here has mainly been concentrated on the successful countries, but specific attention has been given to some unexpected failures, like those of Belgium, Denmark, France, Germany and the Netherlands, as well as to a more general overview. Broadly speaking, two policy orientations (other than giving top priority to maintaining full employment) can be distinguished. One is the consistent 'cut down the public sector, strengthen the market economy' approach. That has been the shortest and fastest route to mass unemployment. The best examples, both of cause and of effect, are Thatcherite Britain and the Netherlands under the right-wing Christian Democrats Van Agt and Lubbers. Belgium since 1981 and in the first years of the crisis has had a rather similar policy orientation.

Another group of countries has more been characterized by inconsistent and discontinuous policies. Slower to take effect than the previous one, this orientation has also proved a sure road to high unemployment. Denmark, France and Germany under Social Democratic governments are among this group. Actually existing Reaganomics may be seen in this context too. The deflationary governmental stance of 1981 had its foreseeable effect in aggravating unemployment, but an increasing combination of deflationary policies — high interest rates, cuts in civilian public expenditure — with what may be called War Keynesianism, caused public deficits and has kept unemployment at a medium high level.

Other kinds of policies and institutions also weigh upon unemployment. While the German (and Swiss) system of vocational training and of wide-ranging apprenticeships have kept youth unemployment relatively low, the much less practically oriented educational systems of France and Italy seem to contribute heavily to the very high youth unemployment in these countries. General sexist social relations and a very limited supply of part-time jobs have been effective in bringing about the very high over-unemployment of women in Belgium, France and Italy. While there is no general relationship between unemployment compensation and unemployment levels (and increase), it seems likely that the type of unemployment compensation affects the structure of unemployment. Generous eligibility rules and unlimited duration seems to have contributed to permanently registered unemployment in Belgium for instance (most probably not as an alternative to employment but as a withdrawal from, or non-entry into, the labour force).

These policy orientations have, of course, worked themselves out in variable contexts of pressures and constraints. The Dutch unemployment disaster in the 1980s, for example, was largely a consequence of the establishment of consistently deflationary policies, a rapid growth of the labour supply in the first years of the decade, the trough of the international business cycle, and the progressive weakening of Dutch manufacturing. Strong growth of the labour force has also been important in Canadian and US unemployment. Like the British case, Belgian unemployment is firmly rooted in a specific, national crisis-generating structure, of the dominance of finance over industry, high import elasticity, rigid labour markets, and an important sector of ailing old industries. The radical misfit between the type of reflationary policies pursued by the Mitterrand government in its first years and the real problems of the French economy comes out very clearly. West Germany seems to have already embarked upon a new pattern of accumulation and development in the mid-1960s, combining vigorous export performance and a truncated development of her domestic economy, with a relatively small service sector and a uniquely falling rate of labour-force participation. That Germany is the home base for discussions about 'the crisis of work society' and Italy and France — with their exclusivist unemployment structures alongside relatively high real wage increases for those employed —

are the breeding-ground of theses of class fragmentation should come as no surprise. Nor should they be taken to express general, international trends.

The Political Lesson: Two Future Perspectives

Mass unemployment is not a fatality, a necessary effect of 'anonymous and evil forces' of contemporary capitalism — it is an inherent potentiality of capitalism. But without the willing or unconscious support or strategic acceptance of right-wing politicians and economic advisers and of faint-hearted or weak-willed Social Democrats and, sometimes, of starry-eyed trade unionists, credulously buying the liberal arguments, high unemployment could have been staved off. And it has been prevented in five of sixteen countries under review.

For the ten countries in which high unemployment is becoming permanent — Finland does not seem as yet to be definitively set on the course to permanent unemployment — the findings of this book indicate two possible future perspectives. The first one we may call the *Brazilianization of advanced capitalism.* The basis of this scenario is our historical explanation of current variations in rates of unemployment. Only those countries in which a commitment to full employment had been historically deeply rooted could muster the force to withstand the onslaught of the crisis. Others failed, even if they wanted to resist, as did initially, the Dutch Social Democrats in the 1970s or the French Social Democrats in the early 1980s. The failures of the progressive forces in the high unemployment countries have demoralized them and encouraged the right, which outside Japan and Switzerland, either does not care about unemployment, or indeed, actually wants it.

Against this background, mass unemployment is likely to become a permanent feature of most advanced capitalist countries, somewhat reduced in years of boom, higher in years of recession and probably with a rising trend. This would produce a society like a richer and somewhat more humane Brazil, with increasing trichotomous socio-economic divisions. At the bottom will be the permanently and the marginally unemployed, with certain welfare entitlements which are almost certain to be reduced over time. Some of these people will make a living in the black economy. In a country like the Netherlands, where social assistance and unemployment benefits are still relatively generous, some will initially adapt to a position of supported marginality (a few perhaps drawing some comfort from proponents of the ideology that the unemployed are pioneers of a happy exodus from 'the work society'). After a period, however, benefits will be reduced, social controls will be tightened, marginality will become exhausting. Desperation and passivity will both grow, breeding riots, repression and contempt.

In the middle there will be the stably employed, or those with the possibility of re-employment, who will probably be increasingly divided according to enterprise, sector and hierarchical position. They will make a fairly decent living, no more, but will be able to congratulate themselves on the widening distance between themselves and the unemployed.

The marginalization of a significant part of the former and the potential working class has already gone hand in hand, in the first half of the 1980s, with increasing wealth and incomes of capitalists and top business managers. They constitute the third layer of mass unemployment societies. Their distance from the plain employed folk has already widened in Britain, the USA, the Netherlands and Belgium. Politically, this ruling class will appeal to the bulk of employees as the guarantors of the latter not falling into the abyss of unemployment, and they will invite the citizenry at large to a vicarious enjoyment of the success of the wealthy and the beautiful, and to the Western European and North American equivalents of soccer and samba.

This is not only a nightmare. It is a society being envisaged and designed. One need not go to the Reaganite American right to find its blueprint. It was laid out (with some omissions) in the jubilant editorial of *The Times* after Thatcher's second victory. 'Surely this election victory has shown that the tired attempts to invest the phenomenon of unemployment with some statistical morality have not taken in the electors. ... Nevertheless, statistical unemployment is here to stay. It is necessary, therefore, to discover a different language in which to explore the profound changes which will effect the whole pattern of work in society in the 1980s and 1990s.'[15]

The kind of newspeak which *The Times* called for has already come forth. On the last day of 1984, the West German Minister of Labour and Social Affairs, Norbert Blüm, published an article in the business daily *Handelsblatt*, entitled 'On the Right Track in the

Struggle against Unemployment'. Blüm's argument was that the three major economic goals *other than* low unemployment had been reached (i.e., growth, price stability, and a good international balance of payments).[16] In order fully to appreciate the argument of the probably most socially progressive Minister in Bonn today, the reader should bear in mind that since Blüm and his colleagues took over in 1982, German unemployment has increased from 6.1 per cent to 8.0 per cent in 1983 and to 8.4 per cent in the third quarter of 1984 and is expected to stay above 8 per cent at least till 1986.[17] The right-wing way to 'struggle against' unemployment is actually increasing unemployment.

If the Brazilianizing tendencies should stabilize, the only way out of that situation, to an at least minimally egalitarian division of participation in the economic life and extra-labour market activities in Western societies, would be a social cataclysm similar in range and depth (if not in form) to the solution of the mass unemployment of the previous major crisis of capitalism — that of the 1930s. Then there were two effective solutions, the pre-war mobilization of Nazi Germany and the wartime mobilization of the other countries.

There is another scenario, which may also be derived from our analysis. The baseline in this case would not be pre-crisis history, but crisis policies in the low unemployment countries. There are actual policies and experiences which may be learnt from and adapted to different national contexts. There is also an important force which may be put behind such an effort. In the very early 1980s, the labour movement and other progressive forces in the West were, on the whole, on a historical high plateau of strength and influence.[18] Failure to maintain full employment has significantly weakened the labour movement in many countries since then. But there is a renewed combativity in the post-Wilson-Callaghan Labour Party and the post-Schmidt SPD, a returning vitality to Belgian Social Democracy and the Italian Communist Party remains against all odds intact as *the* rallying-force of progressive opinion in Italy. Dutch and Danish unions have taken up industrial action in early 1985. New forces have also come out against the option of the rich man's Brazil — most interestingly, many churches and church leaders. In the British miners' strike, Anglican Bishops came out against the class against class line of Thatcher and the right-wing media. In the US an episcopal committee within the Catholic Church has published a draft programme for employment and social equalization which goes clearly beyond anything that the luckless Walter Mondale (not to speak of Gary Hart) ever wanted to propose.[19]

Furthermore, not all fractions of capital benefit from mass unemployment. Thus Thatcher has been presented with a series of employment-promoting public investment proposals from the Confederation of British Industry, the Institution of Civil Engineers, the building-materials producers, the building employers, and the civil engineering contractors.[20] The Japanese and the Swiss examples may also convince a few enlightened bourgeois that you need not necessarily be a Communist or a left-wing Socialist to take full employment seriously.

There is, then, some reason to envisage a *labour comeback* scenario. What lessons could such a labour comeback draw from the successful and from the failed anti-crisis policies so far? First of all, national roads to full employment are possible, and, given the fragile and mainly rhetorical internationalism of labour parties in office, are the ones most likely to succeed.[21] Second, institutional changes are necessary in order to make policies consistent. In particular, this means that progressive control of the policies of the national bank is required. Reflation geared to investment, direct public investment and incentives to private investment have to be prioritized above boosting consumer demand. Fourthly, active labour-market policy measures, of vocational retraining, public works, and special employment in public services, have to be introduced on a massive scale. Productive capital has to be favoured over financial capital and payments of dividends. The supply of part-time jobs, with full social rights and in co-operation with the trade unions, should be massively increased, and in the short run favoured above the much more difficult and risky road of general reduction in working time. Tax structure should shift from payroll taxes and social contributions to taxes on capital assets and/or value added. The labour movement should commit itself to technological change and job flexibility, under conditions of full employment and non-pollution of the environment, and also to nominal wage moderation, under conditions of rising real wages.

These are policy measures, not a programme for political mobilization. This is not the place for that, and a single scholar, however politically committed, is not well placed to draw up such a programme. However, we can make some remarks. In order to become credible, the progressive parties which have a governmental record of failure to maintain full employment will have to make an open, public self-criticism, pointing out where they went wrong in the past and elaborating the lessons they have drawn from this. Secondly, the goal of full employment has to be envisaged and designed as a goal of participation in the making of society and of individual opportunities. Thirdly, a full employment commitment has to be explicitly related to women's emancipation and geared to providing meaningful, independent, and well-remunerated jobs for women. While there seems to be little reason to believe the puritanical, near-exhaustion-of-the-earth prophets of austerity, a commitment to full employment and technological development should make clear as a *sine qua non* of advance, that pollution of the environment should not increase, but be reduced. Finally, under such conditions, all ideologies which attack the goal of full employment should be relegated to where they belong — explicitly or by implication — in the arsenal of the Brazilian ruling class (which all progressive people in Brazil are fighting, but which tends to spread to the mainlands of advanced capitalism).

The labour comeback scenario outlined above is not a socialist one, and my socialist comrades may ask where socialism comes into all this, if at all. Being a socialist, and not just a professor of political science, I do consider that question to be both legitimate and pertinent. But socialism, seen with the eyes of a realistic historical materialism, is not likely to be achieved in one blow on the day after tomorrow, but will be a complex and contradictory epochal transformation, which has already begun and which, if ever, will take a long time to be brought about. As long as a large part of the (potential) working class is unemployed and marginal-ized, no further advances are likely. People on the dole will not bring about socialism.

The elaborated scientific argumentation of this book gives support to both these contrasting future scenarios for the current high unemployment countries — Brazilianization and a labour come-back. The only thing certain in this context, is that the future is open, never completely determined. Your reactions, you who are now reading this text, are one of the crucial determinants of our future.

I
'Grunemployment' and the Paradoxical Economics of the Crisis

1. The Wilson-Callaghan Thesis and its Disproof

In the 1970s advanced capitalism underwent a shift in economic behaviour, with the simultaneous occurrence of stagnation and rising unemployment, on one hand, and accelerating inflation on the other. International vocabulary was thus enriched by a new word — 'stagflation'. Stagflation undermined (most) economists' assumptions about the basic correlations between economic variables, and thus provided the starting-point for the anti-Keynesian onslaught, in which inflation was singled out as the key policy objective. From a successful control of inflation it was argued, growth and employment would follow. The first spectacular political conversion to this view was that of the British Labour Prime Minister James Callaghan who, in a speech to the Labour Party Conference in 1976, told his (rather sceptical) audience: 'We used to think you could just spend your way out of a recession and increase employment by cutting taxes and boosting government spending. I tell you, in all candour, that the option no longer exists, and that insofar as it did exist, it only worked by injecting bigger doses of inflation into the economy followed by higher levels of unemployment at the next step. The (Labour) *Manifesto* was right when it said that the first priority of the Labour Government must be a determined attack on inflation.'[1]

That declaration, together with an even blunter one by Callaghan's immediate predecessor Harold Wilson — 'inflation is the father and mother of unemployment' — was enthusiastically adopted as a battle cry by the Thatcherites. Callaghan and Wilson were both cited as witnesses for the prosecution by the principal ideologue of what later acquired the name of Thatcherism, Sir Keith Joseph, in his very important and influential pamphlet *Conditions for Fuller Employment.*[2]

In a television debate on unemployment on BBC 1 on 11 February 1985, the Callaghan declaration was presented to the viewers on a placard brought to the studio by Norman Tebbit, the toughest Thatcherite after Thatcher herself in the Tory Cabinet. By the mid-1980s, the results of the turn in policy and economic doctrine, inaugurated in Britain about a decade ago and later pursued with much more consistency and ruthlessness than the luckless figures Callaghan and Carter could ever muster, are clearly visible. These results call for a new concept, capable of conveying the association of economic growth and unemployment characteristic of the present period. I have therefore coined the term '*grunemployment*', its jarring sound serving to remind us of the terrible experience it represents. Growth and recovery have become linked to permanent and even rising mass unemployment; inflation, however — despite Messrs Callaghan and Wilson's pronouncements — has fallen significantly. The world of the 1970s has disappeared, and its doctors seem to be caught redhanded inflicting new and deeper wounds on their patient.

Inflation exhibits a declining trend since 1975, a tendency which overrides cyclical ups and downs. The changes in political

Table 1

Percentage Rates of Growth, Inflation and Unemployment in Sixteen[a] OECD Countries 1973-84[3] (Unweighted Averages)

	1973	1975	1976	1982	1984
	Peak	Trough	Peak	Trough	Peak
Growth	5.7	− 0.3	4.3	−0.5	3.4
Inflation	8.4	12.1	9.6	8.6	4.7
Unemployment[b]	2.6	3.9	4.2	7.0	7.8

a) All the major and most developed OECD countries, for which standardized unemployment data are available, or, in the case of Denmark, for which roughly comparable unemployment data exist. For a complete list, see Table 3 below.

b) Countries for which OECD standardized unemployment rates exist only, thus excluding Denmark.

economy that happened in the mid-1970s have not been without effect. But the crisis is deepening. Overall economic growth is following a downward trend, each cyclical peak is lower than its predecessor, each trough is lower than the one before. Finally, unemployment is rising, over and above cyclical variations — indeed, at the business-cycle peak of 1984 it was higher than in the deep trough of 1982. Recovery has ceased to bring about a reduction in the general rate of unemployment. The paradox of the 1970s was that increasing unemployment went hand in hand with rising inflation. The paradox of the 1980s is that overall economic recovery is accompanied by an average increase in the percentage of the labour force out of work.

The Wilson-Callaghan Thesis has been proved wrong. The curbing of inflation has not meant a reduction of unemployment, which has actually risen. This does not imply, however, that the simple boosting of consumer demand, associated with Keynesianism, provides a solution. The stagflation of the 1970s remains a historical fact, and below we will see that the trade-off between inflation and unemployment is hardly the key to the current crisis, as the Philips Curve would suggest. Nor do we face a new stage of advanced capitalism with the combination of growth and mass unemployment as its general defining characteristic. More straightforwardly, we are not living through a rapid technological revolution, which is inexorably creating mass unemployment. Instead one and the same worldwide crisis is having *divergent* effects, above all with regard to unemployment.

2. The Divergent Effects of the Crisis

The onset of the present crisis led to greater variations of growth and inflation. But, since the mid-70s, the various countries' growth and inflation rates have drawn closer together, while rates of unemployment have continued to diverge. Some peoples are, in fact, becoming much more unemployed than others.

The wide and increasing spread of internationally standardized rates of unemployment demonstrates that the present crisis is not a relentless, universal density, unamenable to human agency, and that mass unemployment is not an intrinsic feature of contemporary developed capitalism. But before we draw any conclusions from this, we should sort out the sheep from the goats.

Table 2
The Differential Impact of the Crisis. The Dispersion of Growth.
Inflation and unemployment among sixteen OECD
countries 1973-1984.[4] (Per cent)

	1973	1975	1976	1982	1984
Growth					
Difference between 3 highest and 3 lowest	4.4	7.3	4.7	5.7	3.3
Standard deviation[a]	1.6	2.6	2.3	2.0	1.6
Inflation					
Difference between 3 highest and 3 lowest	4.0	11.9	12.0	6.8	5.2
Standard deviation	1.6	4.3	4.0	3.3	1.9
Unemployment[b]					
Difference between 3 highest and 3 lowest	4.9	5.8	5.9	10.3	11.4
Standard deviation	1.7	2.1	2.2	3.8	4.2

a) To readers not versed in statistics, I should explain that the standard deviation is a measure of dispersion, which indicates the range above and below the average (given in Table 1) within which two thirds of the cases fall. The other measure gives an idea of the distance between extremes. As we are mainly concerned with absolute differences here, the standard deviation has been used as a measure of distribution. It is, however, sensitive to the size of the mean. Measured by the coefficient of variation, which captures dispersion relative to the mean, unemployment has become more evenly distributed: from a coefficient of 0.66 in 1973, to 0.54 in 1975 and 1984 — a reflection of the very low average in 1973 and the existence of three extreme cases.
b) Denmark, for which no internationally standardized unemployment rate is available, is excluded from the unemployment calculations.

The 1970s shattered the complacency of simple-minded Keynesianism or, to be more precise, of those naive under-consumptionist crisis theories and policies which were to be repeated in the early 1980s in Mitterrandist France. The 1980s have disproved the Wilson-Callaghan Thesis — for while inflation has gone down, unemployment has risen. The lesson drawn, in most countries, from the 1970s was therefore wrong. What conclusion can we now draw, in the mid-1980s? The first and crucial lesson, it

Table 3
Unemployment in Sixteen OECD Countries 1983 and 1984[5]
standardized percentage of the labour force

	1983	1984
High[a]		
Belgium	13.9	14.0
Canada	11.8	11.2
Denmark	10.6	10.3
Netherlands	13.7	14.0
UK	13.1	13.2
Medium		
Australia	9.9	8.9
Finland	6.1	6.1
France	8.4	9.8
Germany	8.0	8.0
Italy	9.8	10.1
USA	9.5	7.4
Low		
Austria	4.1	4.2
Japan	2.6	2.7
Norway	3.3	3.0
Sweden	3.5	3.1
Switzerland	0.9	1.1

a) Defined on the basis of the 1983 figures, the limits being 10 and 5 per cent.

would seem, is that a decade of general crisis has had differential and increasingly divergent effects. It is these effects that have to be explained, so that rational strategies and policies can be chosen. What do Austria, Japan, Norway, Sweden and Switzerland have in common, which sets them off from the rest of the advanced capitalist world? Why is Denmark economically so far behind Sweden? Why has Mitterrandism failed in one of its own top priority areas of policy? What does Britain share with Belgium and the Netherlands?

Anticipating the findings of the extensive empirical tests presented below, I would say that an adequate analysis, and the politically proper response to it, have to be based on an acknowledgement of the *national politics of economics*. Before going any further, I would like to make it plain that this is not an essay in crisis theory. Firstly, we may take the word of Nobel Laureate in Economics James Tobin, that, 'by and large, the economics profession has not developed any powerfully convincing diagnosis of the stagflation which has afflicted the United States and world economies of the past decade.' It would then be rather presumptuous for a political sociologist to claim to have *the* explanation — even if modesty is not always a virtue. Secondly, and more crucially, crisis theories are by nature general, whereas in the perspective adopted here, it is the particularities, of mass or low unemployment, which are the decisive factors. In order to investigate the reasons for the latter, we may very well regard the crisis as an external given, leaving others who are more competent in the field to explain the outbreak of the current crisis. Our primary concern is to elucidate why the same crisis has had, and is having, such different effects in different countries. I will begin by putting a series of variables, singled out by standard economics, or popular economic ideology, to empirical test.

3. National Performances and National Trajectories

How should wide differences in the impact of the crisis upon employment be explained? To what extent can these differences be accounted for by relationships between key variables that hold in all market economies, and to what degree do they depend upon the national context of economic relations? To ask this is not to ask the question that is often put in contemporary political science and sociology: does politics matter? This is because there may be effects of government behaviour upon market developments that operate in *all* economies and, conversely, the main impact of the national framework may be on the economic behaviour of nongovernmental economic actors. Insofar as the behaviour of national economies is affected by specific national institutions, there should be important consequences, both for empirical economic analysis and for politics. For the former, national institutional parameters should be explicitly recognized and taken into account. As far as the general political debate about the economy and about economic policy is concerned, it implies that systematic attention should be paid to the problem of whether or not existing national institutions should be maintained as they are and whether it is possible to change them. By definition, a rise in unemployment depends on changes in the growth of economic output (the national product), in the number of people who want jobs, and in productivity, or the relationship between output and employment. Now, other things being equal, we should expect that the higher the rate of overall economic growth the lower the rate of unemployment will be, and that the larger the increase of the labour supply the higher the proportion of those out of work. We should also expect that changes in economic growth and in the number of people wanting jobs should compensate for each other, so that a low growth rate may be counterbalanced by a low or even declining growth of the labour supply. We should therefore also look into the combined effects of economic growth and fluctuations in the supply of labour.

The rise of unemployment in the present crisis may also be due to alterations in the relationship between output and employment, in other words, changes in productivity. A thesis about the crucial national institutional context of economic developments would gain support, to the extent that the same period of international crisis has led to important national variations in overall productivity. In particular, the national context hypothesis would be strengthened to the extent that there is no general systematic relationship between changes in productivity and patterns of growth or investment. It is often argued that nowadays economic growth and/or investment primarily involves or leads to labour saving rationalizations. If that is true, we should expect unemployment due to increased productivity to be associated with either high growth or high investment or both. (There may, of course, be other invariant market relationships capable of explaining changes in the output/employment ratio.)

A simple first test of the rival hypotheses of invariant market relationships and national institutional contexts would be to look at the relations between, on one hand, the increase of unemployment and, on the other, the development of economic growth and of the labour force.

First of all, let us look at what happened to unemployment in the first decade of the present crisis. The changes do not present quite the same picture as do the figures for 1984 displayed in Table 3. The Netherlands, Belgium, the UK and Denmark still top the list of failures. But the old high-unemployment countries — Canada, Italy and, in particular, the USA — have not done too badly. This suggests that the mass unemployment of today has

Table 4
*Unemployment Increase 1973-1984, Annual Economic Growth 1974-84
and Labour Force Development 1973-1984[6]
Unemployment increase in standardized percentages, economic growth in
percentage growth of GDP volume, labour-force development in per cent.*

	Unemploy-ment	Economic Growth	Labour Force
Australia	6.6	2.6	20.2
Austria	2.7	2.4	5.6
Belgium	11.3	1.7	7.8
Canada	5.7	2.6	33.4
Denmark	9.4[a]	1.7	13.1
Finland	3.8	2.7	15.8
France	7.1	2.2	8.2
Germany	7.7	1.7	0.9
Italy	4.0	2.0	11.9
Japan	1.4	3.9	11.2
Netherlands	11.8	1.6	19.6
Norway	1.5	3.9	20.8
Sweden	0.6	1.7	10.5
Switzerland	1.1	0.5	− 5.9
UK	10.0	1.1	5.7
USA	2.6	2.4	26.4
Averages	5.5	2.2	12.8

a) Non-standardised   b) 1983

Correlations (Pearson's r): unemployment increase–economic growth (excluding Denmark) $r = -0.37$, $r^2 = 0.14$; (incl. Denmark) $r = -0.39$, $r^2 = 0.15$; unemployment increase–labour-force growth $r = 0.01$; multiple correlation unemployment increase–economic growth and labour-force growth (incl. Denmark) $R^2 = 0.22$.

different causes to that which existed before 1973. In the period 1968-73 the average unemployment of the countries under consideration (except Denmark) was 2.5 per cent. Only Italy (5.7 per cent), Canada (5.4 per cent), the USA (4.6 per cent) and the UK (3.5 per cent), lay above this level. At that time, the countries which were later to experience extremely high unemployment, either had an average rate (Belgium) or even — like the Netherlands (1.5 per cent) and Denmark (with a roughly comparable rate of 1.3 per cent for 1970-74) — had particularly low proportions of their labour force out of work.[7]

We also see different patterns of success and failure against unemployment. For example, whereas the Netherlands experienced low growth and a strong increase in the labour supply, Belgium enjoyed growth that was below the average but still rather significant together with a small increase in the supply of labour and the UK had very low increases in both. On the other side, low unemployment has been the record both of countries with extremely rapid growth and either about average (Japan) or clearly above the average labour-force growth (Norway), as well as of the country with both the lowest growth rate and a substantial decline of the labour force (Switzerland).

It is therefore remarkable how little of the immediate increase in unemployment may be accounted for by economic growth and by labour-force growth. The latter explains none of the international variation in the rise of unemployment during the crisis. Economic growth accounts for only fourteen per cent of the variation in unemployment increase among the fifteen countries for which we have standardized comparable data. It may be argued that we should look at tendential changes of growth rates, instead of simply their level in the period under review. Economic growth in 1973-84 has slowed down in every single country compared to the 1964-73 period, but the amount of slowdown explains only one per cent of the increase of unemployment in the later period.

Among the countries with low unemployment, Japan has, on the one hand, maintained the highest growth between 1973 and 1984, and, on the other, suffered the largest absolute decline of growth. Oil and gas-rich Norway has had the second highest

Table 5

The Decline of Economic Growth in 1973-83 as Compared to 1963-73.[8]
Percentage of annual average growth of GDP

Australia	3.3	Italy	3.1
Austria	2.8	Japan	6.0
Belgium	3.3	Netherlands	4.0
Canada	3.4	Norway	0.5
Denmark	2.9	Sweden	2.4
Finland	2.3	Switzerland	3.7
France	3.2	UK	2.3
Germany	2.9	USA	2.3

Correlation: Unemployment increase 1973-84−decline of economic growth 1963-73/1973-83: $r = 0.12$, $r^2 = 0.01$.

growth rate and by far the smallest absolute tendential decline. Switzerland has experienced the third largest fall in the rate of growth while Sweden and Austria are just below the average at three per cent. Among the high-unemployment countries both the Netherlands and Belgium have undergone powerful reverses. The tendential declines of both Denmark and, in particular, the UK have been below the average. In terms of growth, the USA has faced the storm of the crisis relatively well and has been less badly hit than either Japan or Germany, despite the fact that both of those economies continue to enjoy faster absolute growth. Denmark and Sweden, which are at the two poles of unemployment increase, have about the same pattern of GDP and labour-force development.

Growth in output and expansion of the labour force explain only 22 per cent of the variations in unemployment increase. The rest, 78 per cent, is due to alterations in the relationships between output and employment. These figures strongly indicate that national economies and national politico-economic systems have behaved very differently in the crisis and have met the challenge of rising unemployment in a number of different ways. Standard text-book economics — and ideological extrapolations from it — seems to be of little help in grasping today's economic problems.

Let us now see what unemployment increase in individual countries could be foreseen on the basis of overall economic growth and labour-force development and how that compares with the actual increase.

There are four extreme cases in our table below. In Belgium and the Netherlands, unemployment has risen much more than could have been predicted from the growth of output and labour supply. In Sweden and Switzerland the opposite is the case. The UK and the USA are mirror images of each other's situation. In the former there is higher unemployment and a larger output employment ratio, in the latter there is lower unemployment and a decline of overall productivity. Four of our low unemployment countries have a smaller rise of unemployment than their output and labour supply would lead us to expect, but so also have two of the three pre-crisis high unemployment countries, the USA and Italy. While the USA has had a lower than average tendential decline in economic growth (Table 5), Italy has had a slightly steeper decline than the average. If we put Danish figures into the estimation model, we find that Danish unemployment shows a similar pattern

Table 6
*Unemployment Increase 1973-84 Predicted and Unexplained by
Economic Growth and Labour-Force Growth[9] Percentage points*

	Predicted	Unexplained
Australia	5.3	1.3
Austria	4.0	−1.3
Belgium	6.0	5.3
Canada	6.9	−1.2
Denmark	6.6	2.8
Finland	4.5	−0.8
France	4.8	2.2
Germany	5.1	2.6
Italy	5.7	−1.7
Japan	1.2	0.2
Netherlands	7.6	4.2
Norway	2.3	−0.8
Sweden	6.3	−5.7
Switzerland	7.1	−6.0
UK	7.1	2.9
USA	6.5	−3.9

'Predicted' refers to the increase in unemployment estimated by the relationship between economic growth and expansion of the labour force on the one hand, and rise in unemployment on the other. 'Unexplained' unemployment increase is the difference between the predicted chance and and the actual one (which can of course give a negative figure). Technically, the prediction is based on the regression equation $U = 9.03 - 0.246 + 0.01L$ and the 'unexplained' column gives the residuals for each country.

to that of Britain.

There has been a general tendency for investment to decline in the course of the crisis and the differential development of investment accounts for slightly more of the difference in the unemployment record of the various countries than output and labour supply do — 26 per cent as opposed to 22 per cent. But most of the variation remains unexplained. Also remarkable is the fact that changes in output/employment ratios — the 'unexplained' increase in unemployment of Table 6 — are hardly related at all to investment trends. In other words, the rise of unemployment cannot be attributed to any general pattern of labour-saving investment in the present period.

Table 7
Gross Capital Formation 1973-83[10] (average annual change in per cent)

Australia	0.7	Italy	−0.4
Austria	−0.0	Japan	1.9
Belgium	−1.2	Netherlands	−1.6
Canada	1.3	Norway	2.0
Denmark	−3.3	Sweden	−0.6
Finland	0.9	Switzerland	−0.4
France	0.5	UK	−0.3
Germany	0.2	USA	0.6

Correlations: Unemployment increase−gross capital formation, $r = −0.51$, $r^2 = 0.26$; productivity changes (unemployment not explained by economic growth and labour force growth)−gross capital formation, $r = −0.20$, $r^2 = 0.04$.

labour-saving investment in the present period.

We may conclude that the evidence so far gives strong support to the hypothesis that variations in contemporary unemployment are mainly due to specific national systems of political economy, rather than supporting the standard economic argument that stresses universal market relationships.

At this point, it would seem appropriate to summarise national economic performances during the crisis. We will take increases in unemployment and per capita growth — both central to people's lives and experiences — as our basic criteria. In this writer's opinion, inflation is not on a par with the two others as a measure of an economy's performance. However, that is an unconventional view, and though left and right usually give inverse priority to unemployment and inflation, the latter is generally accepted as a criterion for evaluating macroeconomic management and performance.

The main difference produced if we assess growth on a per capita basis rather than simply in terms of absolute value is a deterioration in the position of the USA, Australia and Canada and an improvement in the situation of Germany. The extremely low per capita growth in Switzerland shows that exporting unemployment by expelling immigrant workers — a subject we will return to — is not a painless operation for the natives themselves.

Table 8
Economic Performance in the Crisis: Unemployment Increase,
Annual GDP Growth and Inflation.[11]
Unemployment: percentage increase 1973-1984; growth and inflation:
average annual rates 1973-83.

	Unemployment	Growth	Inflation
Australia	6.6	2.6	10.7
Austria	2.7	2.4	6.0
Belgium	11.3	1.7	8.0
Canada	5.7	2.6	9.0
Denmark	9.4	1.7	10.2
Finland	3.8	2.7	11.4
France	7.1	2.2	10.9
Germany	7.7	1.7	4.6
Italy	4.0	2.0	16.2
Japan	1.4	3.9	7.3
Netherlands	11.8	1.6	6.1
Norway	1.5	3.9	9.3
Sweden	0.6	1.7	10.0
Switzerland	1.1	0.5	4.2
UK	10.0	1.1	12.9
USA	2.6	2.4	8.1
Average	5.5	2.2	9.2

Correlation: (excluding Denmark): unemployment increase–average inflation $r = 0.03$.

Inflation has also sometimes been invoked as a cause of unemployment — as in the Wilson-Callaghan Thesis of the 1970s. We have therefore also calculated the correlation between the increase in unemployment and average inflation and found that, in a comparative perspective, there was virtually no relationship between the two.

Half seriously, we can go on to calculate a performance score for the different countries. How our three criteria above should be weighed is arbitrary from a scientific point of view, but let us give them equal weight and use ranking numbers on each criterion. The best performer in each category would thus score 1, the worst 16.

Table 9
Ranking Scores of Crisis Performance[12]

	Unemployment + Growth[a]	Unemployment + Growth + Inflation[b]
Japan	5	11
Norway	5	12.5
Finland	10.5	24.5
Sweden	11	22
France	15.5	23.5
Germany	16.5	18.5
Italy	16.5	32.5
Switzerland	17	18
USA	19	26
Canada	20	29
Denmark	21.5	33.5
Belgium	22	27
Australia	25	38
UK	26	41
Netherlands	31	35

a) For example, the country with the smallest increase in unemployment scores 1 as does the country with the highest rate of growth per capita. Continuing these two rankings gives us a possible range of scores from 2 to 32.

b) Here, for example, the country with the lowest annual rate of inflation scores 1. Combining the three rankings gives us a range of possible scores from 3 to 48.

In order to satisfy both right and left we will make two indices, one exclusive and one inclusive of inflation.

On the three-part index, the five low-unemployment countries fare very well, all coming in the first six positions. On the whole, then, despite considerable variation, combating unemployment also yields a better overall performance record. By contrast, all of the mass-unemployment countries are overall failures, with the exception of Belgium. As we will see below, the structure of Belgian unemployment has a particular character, although, as will appear in Part Three this is also related to careless economic policies.

4. World Market Exposure and National Independence

We have seen that the differential effects of the present crisis on national rates of unemployment cannot be attributed to variations in economic growth and in the size of the labour force. Nor is there any simple and straightforward explanation of changes in output/ employment ratios which we might derive from rates of growth and investment. We also found that no connection remains between inflationary developments and unemployment. In the rest of this first part of the book we shall look at a few other general features of market systems as possible explanations for international differences in unemployment.

One obvious contender is the extent to which a state's dependence on the world market exposes it to crisis. Since the crisis is international, it may well be expected, that the more dependent a country is, the higher the impact of the crisis on unemployment. Given the disrupting effects of the two 'oil shocks' in the mid-1970s and in the early 1980s, it might also be suggested that the more oil a country needs to import, the harder it will be hit by the crisis.

However disturbing the so-called oil shocks may have been, they seem to have had no importance for variations in unemployment. On the other hand, dependence on the world market does have a certain impact. Translating statistics into ordinary language, we can say that 28 per cent of the variation in unemployment may be due to differences in the national importance of world trade. That is not very much, as is clear if we consider that an ad hoc selection of countries could either give the impression that exposure to the world market plays a decisive role — if Belgium, the Netherlands, Switzerland and Sweden were chosen — or no role whatsoever — if Denmark, Switzerland, Austria and Germany are picked out. A further point, which comes out very strongly from these figures is Japan's low level of dependence on foreign trade. The Japanese have been, and are, formidable exporters, but what happens to unemployment is more the result of domestic demand and economic policies, than a consequence of export promotion. We shall examine Japanese domestic economic policy more closely below. On the whole, export performance has no relationship to national differentials in unemployment.[14] The correlation between the increase in unemployment from 1973 to 1984 and the rise in export volume over the 1973 to 1983 period

Table 10
World Market Dependence[13]

	Merchandise Exports and Imports as %of GDP in 1982	*Oil Net Imports% of GDP in 1981*
Belgium	133.0	5.3
Netherlands	94.5	4.0
Norway	58.2	−7.1
Denmark	57.6	4.9
Switzerland	57.1	3.7
Sweden	55.1	4.7
Finland	54.8	6.2
Austria	52.7	4.1
Germany	50.5	4.2
Italy	45.6	6.3
Canada	44.8	1.2
UK	42.0	−1.0
France	39.4	4.4
Australia	30.6	1.6
Japan	25.7	5.2
USA	15.4	2.6

Correlations (excluding Denmark): Trade dependence–unemployment increase, $r = 0.52$, $r^2 = 0.28$; oil imports–unemployment increase, $r = 0.06$, $r^2 = 0.0$

is $−0.11$, $r^2 = 0.01$.

While the relations of various countries to the world market and their performance in it do not bear very heavily upon variations in national rates of unemployment, a case may still be made for the crucial importance of politico-economic national independence. The five low-unemployment countries — as well as the next best performer, Finland — are all outside the European Community. Crucial aspects of employment policy in the smaller European countries would hardly have been possible had they been members of the Community. Measures include the Norwegian subsidies, Swiss and Austrian immigration policies, and the Swedish competitive devaluation of 1982. As we shall see later, the particular anti-unemployment policies pursued by these countries are all deeply rooted in specific national cultures and institutions. It may further be argued that the relatively low increase in unemployment in the United States is largely due to its unique currency independence. The dollar's role as an international currency makes a heavily deficitary reflation possible, at least in the short term. However, national policy independence should not be confused with protectionism. Swedish labour market policies, Austrian public sector policies, Norwegian planning for full employment, Swiss concerns with the destabilizing effects of unemployment or the employment policies of Japanese conglomerates, are compatible both with the EEC regulations, and with a vigorous participation in the world capitalist system.

We cannot, therefore, explain very much by invoking dependence on the world market, and export performance does not determine rates of unemployment at all. This does not mean that the world market and foreign balances are not important constraints on national policies, and there are indications that national policy-making autonomy is crucial. But that is more a political than an economic consideration in that it does not require an isolation from the international marketplace.

5. The Ambiguous Structures of Modernity

Countries have encountered the crisis equipped with their different economic structures. Some economies are modern, others are old fashioned; some are fairly rigid, others dynamic. It would be reasonable to suppose that these types of differences would have some consequences for the development of unemployment. Some might argue that the more modern and flexible economies should enjoy lower rates of unemployment; others might favour the opposite case. Almost everyone would be surprised, however, if it turned out that differences in economic structure have little or no effect on the numbers out of work in particular countries.

Perhaps the most obvious indicator of whether or not a country has modernized its economic structure is the size of its service sector, and we could judge whether a country is undergoing a process of dynamic modernization by looking at the rate of growth of its service sector. Between 1975 and 1982, the total number of jobs in the OECD area fell by 1.8 million to 330 million. Over the same period the number of jobs in the service sector rose to

23.5 million.[15] It would be tempting to jump to the conclusion that those countries where the service sector has grown most rapidly over recent years would today be those with the lowest rates of unemployment. A high level of tertiary employment in 1975 could either mean a possible degree of immunity from the risks of unemployment or, conversely, a saturation of the service sector leaving little room for further growth and, consequently, increasing the risks. In fact, none of these hypotheses is borne out by the facts. A large service sector before the onset of the crisis is only slightly positively associated with an increase in unemployment. There is also an association between service-sector growth and lower rates of unemployment, but it is not a very strong one. 28 per cent of the variation among countries in changes in the level of unemployment may be attributed to service-sector growth.

One might also seek explanations relating to economic structure by the individual sector. It would not be unreasonable to expect that countries with a relatively modern industrial sector on the threshold of the crisis would be more successful in maintaining low unemployment. One way of testing this hypothesis is to identify those branches of industry which have suffered the largest job losses in the crisis, together with those which have been the most successful in maintaining employment. We could then compare national industrial structures and see how they relate to unemployment.

Between 1975 and 1982, two major branches of industry suffered a particularly heavy decline in employment; textiles and clothing on the one hand, and basic metals (steel) on the other. The food, drink and tobacco industries however, have managed to keep their 1975 level of employment intact. Food and drink are perhaps not what first comes to mind as indicators of industrial modernity in the last quarter of the twentieth century, but electronics, a more obvious candidate, is a relatively small employer.[16]

Once again, the complexity of structures and paths of development foils any simple attempt at a general explanation. What has happened to manufacturing is clearly less significant for unemployment in the current crisis than are developments in the service sector. Changes in manufacturing employment have had virtually no bearing (4 per cent) on international differences in the rise of unemployment.

It is striking that as far as the restructuring of employment goes, disadvantageous job structure in 1975 has had no across the board

Table 11
Service-Sector Size, Service-Sector Growth and Unemployment[17]

Unemployment	Service Sector in 1974 Civilian Employment (per cent)	Growth of Service Employment 1975-82 Average annual growth rate (per cent)
High		
Belgium	55.1	1.4
Netherlands	57.5	1.5
UK	54.9	0.7
Canada	63.1	2.7
Denmark	56.0	1.3
Average	57.3	1.5
Medium		
Italy	43.2	2.7
Australia	58.0	2.2
USA	63.4	2.8
France	49.8	1.8
Germany	45.3	1.1
Finland	47.7	2.0
Average	51.2	2.1
Low		
Austria	46.8	1.9[a]
Sweden	56.3	2.3
Norway	55.3	3.6
Japan	50.1	2.2
Switzerland	48.9	1.1
Average	51.5	2.0

a) 1975-1981

Correlation: Service Sector size–unemployment increase, $r = 0.17$, $r^2 = 0.03$; service sector growth–unemployment increase, $r = 0.53$, $r^2 = 0.28$

effect upon changes in employment in the crisis. This can be seen by comparing Belgium and Britain on the one hand, with Italy and Japan on the other. In the Italian case, this is largely because of the uniquely large textile and clothing sector which has maintained an unparalleled level of employment (with an index figure of 96 for

Table 12
Manufacturing and Unemployment[18]

Unemployment 1983	Manufacturing Employment 1975 Percentage of all Civilian Employment	Growth of Manufacturing Production 1975-83 1975=100	Manufacturing Employment Structure 1975[a]	Manufacturing Employment 1975-83 1975=100
High				
Belgium	34.2	113[b]	−18.1[c]	78[b]
Netherlands	24.5	115	3.2	77
UK	30.9	91	−10.2	68
Canada	21.6	111	na	83[d]
Denmark	19.7	127	6.5	90
Medium				
Italy	29.7	118	−20.8	97[b]
Australia	23.3	100	na	(92)[e]
USA	22.7	128	−10.1	88
France	27.9	112	−11.8	97
Germany	35.8	114	− 8.9	90
Finland	28.3	131[b]	na	na

Low				
Austria	30.7	120	na	88
Sweden	28.0	101	− 5.3	77
Norway	24.1	96	− 2.4	87
Japan	25.8	140[b]	−15.8	95
Switzerland	33.7	108	na	89
Average (unweighted)	25.6	114	− 8.5	88

a) Food industry minus textiles and basic metals.
b) 1982.
c) A minus sign indicates how much larger was the employment share of the two branches of industry that, internationally, lost jobs, compared to the share of the branch that was most successful in maintaining jobs.
d) February 1983 (seasonally adjusted).
e) 1980-81 (approximately calculated).

Correlations: Manufacturing equipment 1975−unemployment increase 1973-84, $r = 0.04$, $r^2 = 0$; manufacturing employment 1975-83−unemployment increase, $r = 0.21$, $r^2 = 0.04$.

1982 as compared to an (unweighted) average for the countries analyzed of 81). But Japan has kept low overall unemployment and a relatively high level of manufacturing employment, while massively restructuring her industrial employment. Employment in textiles and clothing fell to a level as the index of 84 in 1982, basic metals fell to 83 (average 77), and wood and furniture to 75 (average 88). At the other extreme, the extraordinarily advantageous position in manufacturing employment in 1975 of the Netherlands and Denmark has not prevented these countries from becoming countries of mass unemployment and, in the Dutch case, from being a less than mediocre performer in manufacturing employment.

It is successful restructuring, rather than initially advantageous structure, which explains the success stories of Italy, Japan and, until 1982, the US (textile and clothing employment index in 1982, 85; basic metals, 77). Furthermore, contemporary unemployment has, in fact, little connection with technical development.

The extraordinary robotization of Swedish industry must have had some negative effects upon manufacturing employment, but it is clear that the relationship between high technology and employment is fundamentally ambiguous. The theory that unemployment is the inevitable consequence of technical change is dead and should be buried.

Again the unemployment of nations resists explanation by any general relationship. The service sector and 'post-industrialist' tendencies have not — or only to a limited extent — accounted for

Table 13
Industrial Robots and Unemployment[19]

	Robots per 10,000 Employed in Manufacturing in in 1981	Manufacturing Employment Growth 1975-1983	Overall Unemployment in 1983-84
Sweden	29.9	Weak	Low
Japan	13.0	Strong	Low
Germany	4.6	Average	Average
USA	4.0	Strong	Average
France	1.9	Strong	Average
UK	1.2	Weak	High

current unemployment patterns. Even less important, internationally speaking, have been manufacturing structures and processes of 'de-industrialization' (taken as general tendencies). The scanty evidence on automation available lends no support to any technological explanation of why some peoples are much more unemployed than others. The uneven development of unemployment in the current crisis can hardly be explained by the arrival of a new stage of advanced capitalism.

Finally, we should take a look at two central theses of fashionable right-wing liberalism — apart from the tenet that inflation is the 'father and mother of unemployment', a notion already relegated by empirical evidence to the dustbin. First, broad conservative opinion asserts that labour cost is a key factor in the creation of unemployment. We shall test that proposition together with a second argument — around which left-wing as well as right-wing currents often congregate — which states that, in capitalist societies, the rate of unemployment is crucially determined by the rate of profit.

6. Labour Costs Explain Nothing and Profits Explain Very Little

From general economic considerations the idea that differences in the cost of labour may account for differences in unemployment is quite plausible. In the Netherlands, and on the political right in Britain and other countries, labour costs figure as a major cause of unemployment. Other things being equal, the argument does make sense, but the question here is precisely whether things are equal across national economies.

Two conclusions emerge strongly from Table 7. Firstly, changes in labour costs have not at all determined the diverging pattern of unemployment rates in the current crisis. Secondly, local currency cost developments have nothing to do with relative costs, measured in a common currency. In the post-Bretton Woods system of floating currencies, currency and monetary policy can make and unmake local incomes policies. The implications of these findings for trade-union and progressive government policy are far-reaching.

The surprising fact that mass unemployment countries have a

Table 14
Labour Costs and Unemployment[20]

Unemployment 1983	Manufacturing Unit Labour Costs 1983 Index 1970 = 100	
	In Local Currency	*Relative Costs in Common Currency*
High		
Belgium	189	74
Netherlands	179	93
UK	471	126
Canada	275	105
Denmark	264	86
Average	276	97
Medium		
Italy	615	103
Australia	no data	no data
USA	203	81
France	336	100
Germany	183	109
Finland	392	121
Average	346	103
Low		
Austria	205	115
Sweden	294	78
Norway	325	131
Japan	173	114
Switzerland	172	143
Average	234	116

Correlations: Unit labour costs in national currency–unemployment increase 1973-83, $r = -0.04$, $r^2 = 0.00$; unit labour costs in international currency–unemployment increase, $r = -0.37$, $r = 0.14$; labour costs in national currency–labour costs in common international currency, $r = 0.15$, $r^2 = 0.02$.

more favourable competitive cost position than low unemployment countries should perhaps be interpreted as an effect of a built-in stabilizer in the new international currency system, in the sense that the currency of weaker economies is being weakened, which tends to enhance their competitive position. However, it has to be emphasized that the competitive cost position of today's mass unemployment countries was already a fact in 1980, before the employment catastrophe of 1981-82. In 1980, the average manufacturing unit labour cost (in common currency) for the fifteen countries (Australia excepted) for which data are available was 114 (1970=100). Four of the five subsequent mass unemployment countries were below that average — Belgium at 101, Netherlands at 103, Canada at 85, and Denmark at 96. Only Britain stood out, at 141. But the British exception was as much a product of currency policy as of domestic managerial inefficiency and wage increases. If currency policy had reduced British labour costs as much as Italian policy did with Italian unit labour costs, British relative labour costs would have stood at 97 in 1980.[21] However, because of the importance and the controversial nature of the issue, we shall put our initial conclusion to a further test. It seems that in most cases 'unit labour costs' only cover wages, but in several countries social security contributions are also a very important cost component. We shall therefore take them into account also. Secondly, the linkage between cost developments in manufacturing and in the rest of the economy may differ considerably between countries, and this makes the use of the former as an indicator of general labour cost developments hazardous and weakens the argument about relations between labour costs and overall unemployment, since manufacturing accounts only for a minority of total employment. In order to check the tenability of our findings in Table 7, we shall then relate total manufacturing labour costs directly to changes in manufacturing employment. Later we shall look into available data for the service sector. For the manufacturing sector in the current period, the verdict is unquestionable. The development of (un)employment has become completely disassociated from changes in labour cost.

The evidence with regard to services points in the same direction. True, if the USA is compared with the major countries of Western Europe (Germany, France, the UK and, in part, Italy), support for the labour-cost thesis may be found in service-sector developments. Real labour costs in private services in the USA decreased by 2.8 per cent over the total period between 1973 and 1981, while employment (of the whole non-manufacturing economy) went up by 28.4 per cent. For the European countries, the corresponding figures were 18.6 per cent and 10.5 per cent

62

Table 15
Total Labour Costs and Employment in Manufacturing 1977-1983[22]

	Average Annual Costs Change 1977-82. Per Cent in Local Currency and Real Prices Per Hour	Employment in 1983 Index: 1980 = 100
Belgium	0.7	89[a]
Netherlands	0.2	87
UK	2.5	82
Canada	0.3	87[b]
Denmark	−0.1	92
Italy	0.5	94[c]
Australia	2.8	98[b]
USA	−0.5	88
France	3.4	93
Germany	2.1	88
Finland	1.3	100[b]
Austria	1.3	90
Sweden	0.0	87
Norway	−0.4	92
Japan	1.4	102
Switzerland	1.1	94

a) 1982 and including mining.
b) 1982.
c) Including construction.

Correlations: Manufacturing Labour Costs–Manufacturing Employment: $r = 0.20$, $r^2 = 0.04$; Manufacturing Labour Costs–Increase in Overall Unemployment 1979-83; $r = 0.01$, $r^2 = 0.0$.

respectively. The picture changes, however, if Japan is brought in. There, private services costs increased by 44.5 per cent, while the non-manufacturing employment increase (which in Japan includes a substantial agricultural sector as well) was almost twice that of Europe at 19.5 per cent.[23] With three cases (the individual major European countries are not distinguished by the OECD), correlations make no sense. But again, we see that for the major OECD countries taken together, labour costs and employment have parted ways.

Economists of almost all persuasions would have us expect that, other things being equal, higher profits would lead to higher

Table 16
Gross Profits and Unemployment[24]

Unemployment Category	Gross Profitability[a] 1982	Trend 1960-82
High		
Belgium	41.4	−1.5[b]
Netherlands	41.2	−
UK	34.7	0.1
Canada	36.0	−0.1
Average	38.3	−0.5
Medium		
Italy	48.3	−0.6[b]
USA	27.6	−0.6
France	39.9	−1.7
Germany	38.0	−0.7
Finland	32.5	−1.0
Average	37.3	−0.9
Low		
Sweden	30.4	−1.0
Norway	47.1	0.3
Japan	38.6	−2.6
Average	38.8	−1.1

a) Ratio of operating surplus to value added, total business sector except financial and farm sectors.
b) Beginning 1970.
c) Beginning 1967.

private-sector employment, smaller profits to lower employment. But how far are things 'equal' and how much of current unemployment can be explained by the level of profits?

Clearly, there is no connection between unemployment and profits, looked at in a comparative international perspective. The trend rather indicates a negative link between profit decline and unemployment. The low profit rate of the USA is remarkable. It changes, however, if we look at gross rates of return (i.e., at operating surplus as a ratio of capital stock). The United States becomes a middle-ranking country, with Japan and Italy showing the highest returns in manufacturing — the sector for which the best data are available — and with Britain, Sweden, Canada, and Norway having the poorest results.[25] In other words, one low unemployment and one medium unemployment country lead the league of returns to capital, and two low unemployment and two mass unemployment countries have the lowest scores. The theory that attributes unemployment to a profit squeeze is discredited.

The fact that neither labour cost developments nor profit levels and profit trends (as available from OECD data) make any important contribution to the explanation of international unemployment patterns, points to the direction of the crucial significance of nationally institutionalized economies. Without denying the importance of labour costs and profit rates for the behaviour of capitalist economies, our findings tend to support the view that variations in unemployment cannot be laid at the door of workers or trade unions making 'excessive' demands. Scientific honesty should lead analysis elsewhere. Let us now turn to another black sheep of contemporary right-wing liberalism, the welfare state.

7. The Failure of the Welfare State and the Error of its Enemies

In the ideological climate of today, the welfare state is more often invoked as a culprit of the contemporary crisis, than as a protector or saviour from it. In fact, the relationship is much more complex. From a right-wing liberal point of view, we should expect unemployment to be positively associated with high taxation and high social expenditure, and economic growth to be inversely related to the latter. Table 17 looks into the cards of the anti-welfare state right.

The evidence is unambiguous, unemployment levels and unemployment increase are associated neither with levels nor with growth rates of taxation or social expenditure. From a working-class point of view this is an indictment; welfare states do not necessarily bring full employment (policies). In view of right-wing accusations, however, the only fair sentence is acquittal. Taxation and social expenditure cannot be held responsible for either high unemployment or for increases in unemployment.

Unemployment compensation is an aspect of the welfare state which has a particular relevance in this context. Conventional economics would have us expect that countries with generous unemployment compensation would tend to have higher

Table 17
Taxation, Social Expenditure and Unemployment[26]

Unemployment Category 1983	Taxation 1982 Including Social Security Contributions	Social Expenditure 1981[a] Percentage of GDP
High		
Belgium	45.4	29.9
Netherlands	55.8	28.9
UK	43.7	17.8
Canada	39.0	15.3
Denmark	50.7	25.6
Average	46.9	23.5
Medium		
Italy	41.5	22.7
Australia	34.4	13.0
USA	32.0	15.3
France	46.9	23.8
Germany	45.3	26.3
Finland	39.7	19.7
Average	40.0	20.10
Low		
Austria	46.7	23.9
Sweden	59.7	26.8
Norway	52.8	21.0
Japan	30.2	12.5
Switzerland	33.2	14.5
Average	44.5	19.7

a) Public social insurance, care and assistance, health care. Figures include transfers, public consumption and public investment.

Correlations: Unemployment 1983–taxation 1982, $r = 0.13$, $r^2 = 0.02$; unemployment 1983–social expenditure 1982, $r = 0.32$, $r^2 = 0.10$; tax increases 1973-82–unemployment increase 1973-83, $r = 0.05$, $r^2 = 0.00$; social expenditure increase 1973-81 (in 1970 prices)–unemployment increase 1973-84, $r = 0.25$, $r^2 = 0.06$.

unemployment than those with more restrictive benefits. Comparable data on unemployment benefits are difficult to find and to compile, because, on the one hand, there are different categories of unemployed and, on the other, the rules regulating entitlements to different categories vary considerably across countries. However, by putting together three sets of data, we should be able to give the disincentive hypothesis a fair test.

The broadest data collection has been done by the UN Commission for Europe, providing information about income replacement ratios net of taxes for manufacturing workers over one year of unemployment (Table 18a).

There is, then, apparently no relationship between the income replacement ratio of unemployment benefits and unemployment. Appealing to people favourable to the welfare state as this conclusion may be, we should not stop at this point. The 'typical worker' whose incomes during employment and unemployment are compared above, is a statistical artefact, a product of the old days of taxation. He is a male married worker with a housewife and two children, and is as such untypical both of the employed and the unemployed today. For two specific groups of countries better information is available. For the seven big countries, two senior members of the OECD Secretariat, A. Mittelstadt and P. Roberti,

Table 18a

Unemployment Benefits Net of Taxes as Per Cent of an Adult Manufacturing Worker's Wage in 1928[27]

Austria	52.2	Italy	19.0[a]
Belgium	67.3	Netherlands	89.4
Denmark	92.0	Norway	69.3
Canada	74.8	Sweden	80.5
Finland	44.0	Switzerland	80.2
France	64.0[a]	UK	47.0
Germany	75.0	USA	63.3

a) Excluding unemployment for 'economic reasons', 90.0 in France and 47.0 in Italy. Such benefits cater for lay-offs among formerly stable employed workers, a small group of the unemployed in these countries.

Correlation: Unemployment benefits 1982–Unemployment 1982; $r = 0.06$, $r^2 = 0.02$. If the higher values for France and Italy are used, r is equal to 0.

Table 18b
*Average Unemployment Benefits and Beneficiaries of Unemployment
Compensation the Seven Big OECD Countries*[28]
*Percentage of average wage in 1980 (or nearest date and percentage of the
unemployed). Countries ranked in order of rising unemployment.*

	Benefits	Coverage	Year of Coverage
Japan	68.9	55[a]	1979
Germany	67.4	42[b]	1983
France	42.9	52	1983
USA	36.3	43	1980
Italy	17.4	38	1980
Canada	42.9	87	1982
UK	32.0	43	1980

a) In 1975 Japanese coverage was 87 per cent.
b) Including (lower) long-term unemployment benefits.

have brought together data both for average benefits actually paid
and of the number of unemployed who actually benefit from
unemployment insurance. It is from these data that Table 18b is
calculated.

Again, there is no relationship between unemployment
compensation and unemployment. On the basis of both tables,
unemployment compensation in the USA emerges as surprisingly
generous compared to many European countries, in particular
Italy and the UK. It is also possible to conduct a useful comparison
for the Nordic countries (Table 18c).

Again no sign of unemployment benefits causing higher
unemployment can be found. After this triple test, popular
economic ideology about employment disincentives can safely be
laid to rest.

The conclusions from this first part are threefold. Firstly, the
current international crisis has so far had increasingly divergent
international effects on unemployment. The gulf between high and
low unemployment countries is widening. Secondly, unemployment has become disassociated from low economic growth, and a
rising trend is asserting itself over business cycle oscillations.
Thirdly, general market relationships seem to explain little or
nothing of the variations in unemployment among advanced

Table 18c
Unemployment Benefits and Unemployment Insurance Coverage in the Nordic Countries in 1982.[29]
Unemployment compensation as a percentage of the average manufacturing wage (in both cases net of taxes). Coverage by percentage of the unemployed. Countries ranged in order of rising unemployment.

| | Benefits as av. man. wage | | Coverage |
	(Adult)	(Unskilled 18-year-old)	%
Norway	59	57	67
Sweden	93	93	61[a]
Finland	43	43/36[b]	77[c]
Denmark	86	89	81

a) Covered by voluntary, trade-union-organized unemployment insurance. Another 17 per cent of the unemployed had a right to unemployment compensation from the state, at a lower level. Figures refer to 1983.
b) The compensation entitlement.
c) 37 per cent of the unemployed are covered by voluntary unemployment insurance, forty per cent by a state-run scheme.

capitalist countries. Instead, the importance of national contexts and institutions appears more and more clearly.

This indicates that an answer to why some people are more unemployed than others should be sought, primarily, either in a general conception of socio-political institutions or in a comparative history of institutions and policies. It will be argued here, that an adequate explanation is to be found mainly along the second path. However, if we suspect that unemployment is not simply a manifestation of general market developments, we should also expect that behind and beneath the standardized rates of unemployment there are particular configurations, both of unemployment and of contributions of employment and unemployment. Before turning to the task of providing an alternative explanation to the 'orthodox' or 'vulgar', popularly propagated economics — which the best of economists hardly take seriously while nevertheless hiding in their well-cushioned retreats of pure theory and models — we shall devote a second part of this book to distinguishing among different national labour market profiles and structures of unemployment.

II
Profiles of Unemployment

The main task of this book is to explain why the present crisis of advanced capitalism has led to higher rates of unemployment in some nations than in others. But to focus simply on *rates* of unemployment would be inadequate. Unemployment is part of a whole complex of social labour-market relations which is irreducible to a supply of labour determined by demography and prices and a demand governed by economics and politics.

1. Rates of Employment and the Status of Work in Society

An important concept that complements the rate of unemployment is the rate of *employment*. This refers to the proportion of the adult population below retirement age who declare themselves to be either employees, employers or self-employed. The concept has yet to become established in research and discussion on the labour market; the notion of 'rate of participation' (the proportion of the adult population in the labour force) has been used instead. With the rise of what seems to be permanent mass unemployment, however, the 'participation rate' loses more and more of its significance. Nevertheless, it is only recently that the OECD has begun to make use of a standard that corresponds to the concept of an employment rate.[1] This is the 'employment/population ratio' — total employment as a percentage of the population between fifteen and sixty-four years of age (Table 19).

Table 19
The Rate of Employment 1975, 1979 and 1983[2]
Total employment as percentage of the population aged 15-64.

	1975	1979	1983
Belgium	61.2	59.6	56.5
Netherlands	54.3	53.4	51.5
UK	71.4	71.0	64.4
Canada	63.5	65.5	64.0
Denmark	73.0	75.1	71.7
Italy	55.5	55.8	54.7
Australia	67.6	65.1	63.1
USA	63.0	67.6	66.1
France	64.5	64.0	60.6
Germany	65.2	64.6	59.4
Finland	70.9	71.1	73.4

These cold statistics have a direct bearing on the other heated debates about the 'crisis of work society', the 'crisis of the work ethic' and about the role and importance of paid work in contemporary and future society.[3]

In the two most important capitalist countries — the USA and Japan — the rate of employment has actually increased during the period of economic crisis. For the postwar era as a whole, participation in the labour market has grown massively, due to the influx of female labour onto the market. In 1950 around 65 per cent of the population between the ages of fifteen and sixty-four participated in the labour force; by the mid-1970s the proportion had risen to 67 per cent. In spite of a slight decline in the rate of employment since 1960, we can safely say that paid work is still at a high point as far as its place in society during the history of capitalism goes.[4] The 'work society', said to be in crisis, is in fact a very recent phenomenon.

The variation in the employment rate among countries is striking. Whereas almost four-fifths of the Swedish adult population are in paid work, the same is true of only just over half of the Dutch people. The advanced countries fall into three groups as regards the significance of (declared) paid work and the rate of unemployment. First of all, there are the Scandinavian countries — Sweden, Norway, Finland and Denmark — which enjoy a high employment rate. Secondly, there are the countries with a very low employment rate — Italy, Belgium and the Netherlands. Finally, we have an intermediate group, which ranges from West Germany with a very low rate to quite high ones in Switzerland and Japan. Japan's high rate of employment is misleading, because of the high level of employment of people aged sixty-five and over. In Japan in 1980 26 per cent of such people worked, compared to 6.5 per cent in Sweden and 12.5 per cent in the USA.[5]

2. Patterns of Gender in Unemployment

Apart from the situation of the labour market and unemployment, the rate of employment is determined by educational requirements and opportunities, the extent to which the sexist division of household labour predominates and the various options available for retirement. The most significant of these influences is the sexist division of housework, measurable by the degree of female participation in the labour force.

In all but two countries — Switzerland and West Germany —

Table 20
Rates of Female Participation in the Labour Force, 1975 and 1983[6]
Employed and registered unemployed as percentage of the population aged 15-64.

	1975	1983
Belgium	43.9	49.4
Netherlands	31.0	38.7
UK	55.3	57.5
Canada	50.0	60.3
Denmark	63.5	72.5
Italy	34.6	40.8
Australia	50.8	52.4
USA	53.4	61.9
France	49.9	52.1
Germany	49.6	49.6
Finland	65.6	73.5
Austria	47.9	50.3
Sweden	67.6	76.6
Norway	53.3	67.0
Japan	51.7	57.2
Switzerland	49.6	48.6

female participation in the labour force has increased despite the crisis. 'This development has been most dramatic in Norway, Sweden, Denmark and the USA. International differences are even more marked as far as sexism is concerned than they are over employment rates. It is possible to distinguish four groups of countries by the degree to which sexism regulates the labour market.

In Italy and Switzerland the differential between the sexes has increased somewhat during the crisis: from 37.8 per cent in Switzerland in 1975 to 41.4 per cent in 1983; in Italy from 39.6 per cent to 40.2 per cent. The gap has narrowed everywhere else. In 1975 the Netherlands was in a class of its own with a differential of 52.2 per cent. The situation has improved somewhat, but

Table 21
Difference in Male–Female Unemployment and Participation in the Labour Force.[7] *(per cent)*

	Participation	Unemployment (1983)[a]
Huge Difference		
Netherlands	41.6	0.5
Switzerland	41.4	−0.2
Italy	40.2	−9.7
Large Difference		
Australia	34.6	−0.7
Austria	32.4	−1.6
Japan	31.9	0.1
Germany	30.4	−1.8
UK	30.4	5.4
Belgium	30.0	−7.9
Significant Difference		
France	27.3	−4.4
Canada	24.7	0.4
USA	22.8	0.5
Norway	19.1	−0.9
Denmark	16.7	−0.8
Fairly Small Difference		
Sweden	9.3	−0.2
Finland	9.2	0.1

a) Minus sign indicates that women have a higher rate of unemployment.

Holland is even further behind Sweden than it was then, as the Swedish differential has narrowed from 21.6 per cent to 9.3 per cent. Unemployment differentials have risen strongly in Belgium, have moved firmly against male workers in the UK and have shifted to the advantage of women in the USA in 1982-3.

3. The Role of Age

The labour market has a very different significance for young people depending on the advanced capitalist country they are in. 67 per cent of British 16-19 year olds were either working or registered unemployed in 1981. The figure was 55 per cent in the USA, 50 per cent in Sweden and only 27 per cent in France. (The high US rate is due to the common North American combination of schooling with part-time work). Japan is at the bottom end of the scale with a participation rate for 15-19 year olds of 17.5 per cent. Among 20-24 year olds the participation rate ranges from 61.9 per cent in Italy to 84.8 per cent in Sweden, with the rate for most countries falling into a 70-75 per cent band. From the early 1960s to 1981, labour-force participation of the 15-24 year old age group increased strongly in the USA and Canada, slightly in Australia, remained stable in Sweden, declined a little in Britain and fell off sharply in Japan, France, Germany and Italy.

The changes in youth involvement or dependence upon the labour market took place in the 1960s, by and large remaining stable in the current crisis. (Registered unemployment is, of course, a form of dependence upon the labour market.) What has changed significantly in the present period, however, is the labour-market involvement of *older males*. In Austria, Belgium, France and Germany the decrease in participation during the 1970s in this group (aged 60-64) has been drastic. By 1979, the rate was 26.1 per cent in Austria (after a decline of 21.6 per cent); 33 per cent in Belgium (in 1981); 38.2 per cent in France, and 39.5 per cent in Germany (declining by 35.2 per cent). Smaller changes took place in Britain (participation rate 75.8 per cent), the Netherlands and Sweden (69 per cent), and the USA (61.8 per cent).[8] In the early 1980s a dramatic exit of older males from the labour market has occurred in some countries. In the Netherlands, for example, labour force participation by males aged 60-64 was down to 42.7 per cent in 1980 and to 39.6 per cent by 1983.[9]

The social position of work in advanced capitalist countries is undergoing three major changes in the current crisis, none of which has much connection with the ideological debate about the 'crisis of work society'. One is a substantial lowering of the actual age of retirement, which, in combination with increased longevity is creating a large layer of people with ten to fifteen years of a (possibly) active life outside the relations of production, having their own specific source of income (pensions). Secondly, labour-market dependence for people of normal working age is being divided into two kinds of position of an increasingly permanent character — that of the employed and that of the unemployed. The third change is that the first two changes take place in some countries, but not, or only to a quite limited extent, in others. For instance, the labour-force participation of older males in Sweden remained fairly stable in the early 1980s for males aged 55-64; it only declined from 78.7 to 77.1 per cent in 1980-83.[10] Not only unemployment but also participation in the labour force is becoming a feature around which the rich capitalist nations diverge from each other.

4. Labour Time

There is a wide variation in the duration of work from country to country. The relevance of working hours to the level of unemployment is, however, less clearly established than much trade-union and left-wing opinion would like to assume. For industrial workers at least, the trend seems to be for a longer working day in the countries of low unemployment, and shorter hours where there is mass unemployment.

Since industrial workers are now in the minority in advanced capitalist countries, it is as well to look at some further data before jumping to any conclusions. However, these figures can also be misleading since the average annual hours worked conceal differences in the distribution of working-time among workers. It is therefore necessary to look at the extent of part-time working in the different economies. Finally, we should look at the changes in the absolutely numbers of those employed.

Definitions of part-time work vary from country to country, so we must be cautious in drawing conclusions. Nevertheless, we can make some assessment. Despite a prevailing scepticism in the

Table 22
Hours Worked by the Average Industrial Worker in 1983[11]

	Normative	Actual
Belgium	1748	no data
Netherlands	1816	1658
UK	1794	(1714)[a]
Italy	1800	1645
USA	1920	1860
France	1771	1651
Germany	1760	1635
Austria	1808	no data
Sweden	1816	1596
Japan	2094	2061
Switzerland	1940	no data

a) Figure for 1978 when the norm was 1864 hours.

Table 23
Change in the Hours Actually Worked per Employee 1975-1982.[12]
1982 situation where 1975 = 100.

Netherlands	90.6	Germany	93.7
UK	89.9	Finland	94.5
Canada	93.3	Sweden	92.8
Italy	96.7	Norway	91.0
USA	(95.2)[a]	Japan	95.7
France	90.0		

a) The US figure is not strictly comparable to the others since it refers to employees only for 1973-1981 and to non-supervisory private-sector workers for 1981-82.

Swedish labour movement about the efficacy of reducing working hours as a weapon against unemployment, it emerges quite clearly that Sweden's low unemployment and high rate of employment is in large part a consequence of the comparatively brief working hours and the widespread nature of part-time employment. Japanese, American and Italian (un)employment patterns, on the other hand, are mainly a consequence of widespread full-time work. The decrease in part-time work in Italy and Britain is

Table 24

Part-time Employment in 1981. Percentage of Total Employment and Percentage Increase since 1973.[13]

	1981	*Increase 1973-81*
Belgium	6.4	3.6
Netherlands	19.4	15.0
UK	15.4	0.1
Canada	13.5	2.9
Denmark	20.8	3.8
Italy	2.7	− 0.8
Australia	15.9	4.5
USA	14.4	0.5
France	7.4	2.3
Germany	10.2	2.5
Finland	4.5	0.6
Sweden	25.2	7.2
Norway	28.3	4.8
Japan	10.0	2.1

Table 25

Changes in Full-time and Part-time Employment 1973-1981.[14] *(1,000s)*

	Full-time	*Part-time*
Belgium	−117	127
Netherlands	196[a]	162[a]
UK	−626	− 86
Canada	1085[b]	485[b]
Denmark	46[b]	112[b]
Italy	2120	−154
Australia	413	393
USA	10,274	2158
France	493	540
Germany	−270	685
Finland	73[c]	17[c]
Sweden	− 18	364
Norway	73[b]	133[b]
Japan	3010	1150

a) 1973-79
b) 1975-81
c) 1976-81

remarkable, as are the very low rates of part-time work in Italy, Finland, Belgium and France.

The maintenance of low unemployment in some countries can hardly be attributed to any reduction in working time. The examples of Norway and Sweden do however suggest that there are possibilities for shorter hours that are untapped in the countries of mass unemployment (it should be borne in mind that Swedish industry is clearly competitive on the world market). The case where average annual working time is cut and there is no appreciable increase in part-time working — the British and French experiences — indicates that labour-time reduction may take different forms, with different implications for both employment and unemployment.

5. The Structures of Unemployment

Behind the overall rate of unemployment, there are significant differences in age and sex distribution and in duration. Let us first look at age differences and in particular at youth unemployment.

Table 26
Youth[a] and Adult Unemployment in 1983.[15]

	Youth	Adult
UK	23.2	8.8
Canada	19.9	9.6
Italy	32.0	4.7
Australia	17.9	7.1
USA	16.4	7.4
France	21.0	5.7
Germany	10.8	7.0
Finland	11.4	5.1
Sweden	8.0[b]	2.6
Norway	9.7	2.1
Japan	4.5	2.4

a) Youth = 15-24; adult = 25 and over
b) Since 1984, when all Swedish youth under twenty were guaranteed either education or a part-time job, this picture has changed.

Everywhere, youth unemployment is higher than adult unemployment. But international differences are stark. Italy has the labour market that discriminates by far the most against youth, with youth employment 6.8 times higher than adult unemployment. The German apprentice system, on the other hand, has resulted in a level of youth unemployment only one and a half times the adult level.

Gender differences are smaller than generational ones, and they also vary in both directions. For the OECD as a whole, female unemployment is higher than male unemployment (8.5 per cent compared to 7.8 per cent in 1983) with a tendency for the gap to narrow in the crisis. Canada, Finland, Japan, the Netherlands and the USA have a slightly higher male rate of unemployment and the UK a considerably higher male rate. In all other countries, it is women who are hit hardest by unemployment. The most sexist distribution of unemployment is found in Italy, a difference of 9.7 per cent between men and women, and in Belgium, where the figure is 7.9 per cent (see table 21 above).

It is therefore not true to say, as a general rule, that women are hit hardest by the current crisis. As we saw in Table 18 above, women have continued to enter the labour market in increasing proportions (except in Switzerland and Germany) and the differential sex incidence of unemployment has rather tended to decrease. In a third of our countries unemployment is actually higher among men than women. Apparently, it takes more than the present economic crisis to stop the advance of (long delayed) female emancipation. But in Belgium and particularly in Italy huge gender and generational divisions significantly affect the way that class structures the labour market. The division of the Italian working class and potential working class is further enhanced by the fact that slightly less than half of the labour force is covered by unemployment insurance.[16] Large-scale unemployment is becoming a permanent feature of two-thirds of the advanced capitalist countries. But the duration of individual unemployment is not the same thing as the duration of a high aggregate rate of unemployment. We must therefore pay special attention to individual experiences in different countries.

Three comments seem appropriate. Belgium stands out as a country of hopelessly long (probably mainly permanent) individual unemployment. In July 1984, 47 per cent of the Belgian unemployed had been out of work for more than two years.[17] In

Table 27
Unemployment for Twelve Months and Over in 1983 as Percentage of Total Unemployment.[18] *(Japanese figure from 1982)*

Belgium	62.8
Netherlands	43.7
UK	36.2
Canada	9.5
Australia	27.6
USA	13.3
France	42.6
Germany	28.5
Finland	14.6
Austria	9.0
Sweden	10.1
Norway	7.0
Japan	14.3

other words, Belgium has created a permanent layer of working-age outcasts from the labour market. Secondly, mass unemployment in Canada is much less serious than in the other countries of labour market failure, due to the greater turnover among the unemployed, a characteristic feature of the Canadian labour market, not only in 1983. On the other hand, the high incidence of long-term unemployment in France points to more serious problems than the overall medium rate of unemployment would suggest.

Unemployment is not all of a piece. It differs widely across nations in terms of how different social categories are exposed to it, in its average duration, and in its economic consequences for its victims (in the sense of direct unemployment compensation). To summarize briefly and provisionally a large set of data, we may distinguish a number of *structures of unemployment*. One type we may call *punitive industrial crisis unemployment*, exemplified mainly by the UK. Male employment is considerably higher than female and largely tied to a profound industrial crisis. Unemployment benefits are relatively low, in particular for single persons, and few unemployed get them (45 per cent in 1980).

A *compensated general crisis unemployment* is found in the Netherlands. There is slightly higher male than female unemployment — related to a more evenly spread economic crisis — and unemployment compensation, despite recent cuts, remains relatively generous with minimum benefits for an adult couple equal to the adult minimum wage.

In Belgium, France and, above all, Italy we have an *exclusivist unemployment*. Unemployment particularly befalls women and youth (to an extent unparalleled elsewhere). Long-term unemployment is very high. Unemployment compensation is also very exclusive in France and Italy, mainly geared to compensating people with long-term prior employment records who are unemployed for 'economic' reasons. In Italy little more than a third of the unemployed get any compensation, which on average is only seventeen per cent of the average wage (in 1980). In Belgium, where unemployment benefits are of unlimited duration and more evenly distributed, we may talk of *compensated exclusivist unemployment*. While France seems to occupy an intermediate position it seems quite proper to speak of *punitive exclusivism* with regard to Italy. The exclusivist unemployment pattern of these countries is also enhanced by their combination of high unemployment with a relatively favourable improvement of real wages for those employed.

Compensated shake-out unemployment may perhaps be used with reference to Canada and Denmark. Relatively little long-term unemployment, a relatively moderate excess of unemployment among youth, and no great difference between male and female rates of unemployment characterize these countries. Unemployment compensation is relatively generous in Denmark and to some extent in Canada. The actual coverage of the unemployed by unemployment insurance is very high, 87 per cent in Canada (highest of all countries), 81 per cent in Denmark (both figures from 1982).

Punitive shake-out unemployment differs from the preceding type mainly with regard to the level of compensation, which is much lower. Australia, Finland and the USA fit into this pattern, although only with qualifications. Australia has a more long-term unemployment than the others in this category. Finland has a relatively wide (70 per cent) coverage for her rather low unemployment compensation, and the USA has a strong streak of racist exclusivism in its labour market, with unemployment hitting Blacks and Hispanics in particular. In 1984 the US unemployment rate for whites was 6.5 per cent, while it was 10.7 per cent for Hispanics, and 15.9 per cent for Blacks.[19]

Germany has *adult exclusivist unemployment*, a unique pattern of unemployment in the sense of a relatively low level of youth unemployment, lower than in any other country of the medium unemployment group, and only half that of France (in 1983). The other side of the coin is that adult unemployment is higher in Germany than in Italy and France. Female unemployment is significantly higher than male, though not as much as in the Latin countries. Unemployment compensation is fairly high (among the seven largest countries, it is second only to that of Japan) but the beneficiaries are relatively few — 42 per cent of the unemployed in June 1983; 65 per cent in 1980 if recipients of the lower unemployment assistance for long-term unemployed are included. While unemployment is not so blatantly an expression of social closure as in Belgium, France and Italy, German unemployment has a clearly exclusivist tinge to it, emphasized by the blocking of the increase of women's participation in the labour force and by the exportation of migrant labour.

Among the low unemployment countries, unemployment is, above all, a youth problem. This is very markedly the case in Norway and (before the 1984 Youth Act guaranteeing part-time employment to everybody under the age of twenty) in Sweden. This is less true of Japan, with more adult unemployed. Gender differences in this category are small (with some exception for Austria). The duration of unemployment is generally relatively short in Norway, Sweden and Austria, longer in Japan (Swiss data are not available at the time of this writing). Unemployment compensation has a relatively wide coverage, and is rather high in Sweden and Switzerland, it is about average in Japan (although highest among the seven big countries) and Norway, and relatively low in Austria. This type of unemployment might perhaps be named *compensated marginal unemployment.*[20]

6. Migration and (Un)employment

An important characteristic of advanced capitalism in the boom period of 1965-73 was the systematic import of foreign labour and the facilitation of international labour migration. The history of this process, which changed the pattern of social relations in many countries, remains unwritten. Indeed, we do not even have standardized, comparable measures of the size of the immigrant labour force. But since the regulation of immigration has played a crucial part in the labour-market policies of a number of countries, thus affecting rates of unemployment or employment, we have to try to make at least some assessment of the importance of migration. Exporting unemployment by forced and/or actively stimulated emigration has been a major policy in Switzerland, Germany, Austria and France. For some countries systematic data are available.

The same numerical data are not available for France. We know only that there was a fall in the number of foreign workers between 1976 and 1979. In spite of the substantial immigration into Britain from the non-white parts of the former empire, continued emigration to the 'Old Commonwealth' has kept Britain as a net emigration country just as before the crisis.[21] Italy has historically been a country of mass emigration, but in the decade 1971-81 there was a small net re-immigration.[22] Finland has also had major emigration in the postwar period mainly to Sweden, culminating in 1969 and 1970, when the population of Finland decreased. In 1971-74 and in the early 1980s, however, there has been a net re-immigration.[23] Denmark and Norway have had a small amount of net immigration in the 1960s and 1970s, but the numbers have been small, and foreign citizens make up only two per cent or less of the labour force.[24] In Japan, a fairly small positive immigration balance before the crisis turned into a negative one in 1976-79, this was significant only in 1978, when the emigration balance was 0.4 per cent of the total population.[25]

Australia, Canada and the United States form part of what used to be called the New World, i.e. countries of immigration. In 1981,

Table 28
Foreign Workers as Per Cent of the Labour Force in 1980.[27]

	Actual	*Assuming the Same Number as in 1974*	*Change*
Austria	5.9	7.0	−1.1
Belgium	8.0	6.7	+1.3
Germany	8.1	8.9	−0.8
Netherlands	4.2	3.3	+0.9
Sweden	5.4	4.6	+0.8
Switzerland	16.6	19.6	−3.0

35 per cent of the Australian labour force was foreign born.[26] That is the highest figure among our countries. The last available Canadian figure, for 1971, tells us that about 20 per cent of the Canadian labour force were born abroad.[28] For the United States, I have been unable to find a corresponding figure, but in 1979 the foreign-born made up 5.4 per cent of the (registered) US population.[29] In all three countries, immigration has continued in the times of crisis, although the number of 'settler arrivals' in Australia declined strongly from 1975.[30] Canada also admitted fewer immigrants after 1974, but the decline was, on the whole, less than in Australia, and as a proportion of total population growth, immigration reached a postwar peak in 1977-82.[31] Immigration into the United States has not abated in the crisis. Indeed, the rate of immigration in the 1970s was the highest since the 1920s.[32] The official statistics do not, for obvious reasons, take into account the illegal immigration. To all appearances, unregistered immigration has increased substantially in recent years.

Now what pattern emerges from these data? The protectionist labour market-policies of the Teutonic lands (Austria, Germany, Switzerland) and, to a lesser extent, France stand out as one pattern. Their opposite is found in the three settler countries, but it is worth noting that the door to immigration has remained open in two of the countries of mass unemployment — Belgium and the Netherlands. Sweden is the only low unemployment country having both a significant proportion of foreign workers and a continuing net immigration.

7. The Growth of Employment and its Patterns

The rise of unemployment does not preclude the possibility of growing employment (lower than the increasing demand for jobs). In fact, in most of the countries under review, the crisis has entailed a growth of employment. Clear exceptions are Switzerland, Germany, Britain and Belgium, where employment has declined. Austria, Denmark and France have had a record of employment stagnation.

As with regard to unemployment, we find here that the crisis has had a diverging impact. On one hand, we have countries with a vigorous growth of employment — Canada, the USA and Norway — and, on the other, those with declining employment —

Table 29
Employment Development 1973-84.[33]
Index 1973 = 100

Belgium	96
Netherlands	107
UK	96
Canada	125
Denmark	102
Italy	108
Australia	112
USA	122
France	101
Germany	94
Finland	111
Austria	103
Sweden	110
Norway	119
Japan	110
Switzerland	93

Switzerland, Germany and Britain. The development of employment is not simply the reverse of that of unemployment. Each of the extremes of employment change happens to contain one country from each of the three employment categories. In contrast to unemployment, however, the employment gap goes back to before the crisis. Total employment in Germany was already declining in the 1960s (0.2 per cent per year in 1960-67), in Britain it began to drop in 1967. Switzerland had a decrease in employment in 1966, but had an employment record more positive than the average for the small European countries in 1967-72. Canada and the USA already had by far the most expansive labour markets in the boom years of the 1960s, but the difference between North America and the rest of the OECD widened considerably in the 1970s. In 1960-67 US employment grew by 1.9 per cent annually, as compared with 0.7 per cent in the rest of the OECD. For the period 1973-80 growth was 2.1 per cent and 0.5 per cent respectively.[34]

The expansion of the American labour market has only recently been brought to public attention and is now often invoked as a positive result of Reaganomics. In fact, the difference between the USA and Western Europe with respect to job creation was largest in the Carter years of 1976-78 and smallest — in recent decades — for the period 1980-82.[35]

Canada, the USA and Italy were alone among our sixteen countries in having a positive growth of manufacturing employment in the 1973-80 period.[36] That trend was broken in 1980. The decline of US manufacturing employment in 1980-83 was 12 per cent compared to 14 per cent in the EEC. Only Japan managed to maintain manufacturing employment in the second trough of the current crisis.[37]

Though it is true that the major part of employment growth in North America has taken place in the service sector, the largest differential for the periods 1960-67, 1973-80 and for the 1960-80 period as a whole, has been in manufacturing employment. With regard to the latter, the difference in growth rates between the USA and the EEC was 2.2, 1.7 and 1.3 per cent points for each of these periods. The differences for the same periods in service sector employment was 0.8, 1.4 and 1.2 per cent. De-industrialization has, overwhelmingly, been a European phenomenon. How is sectoral employment development related to unemployment? By putting together a few available statistics, we may at least get a rough picture.

Apparently, there is no single employment pattern underlying either mass or low unemployment. Instead, there are specific national patterns, some of which seem more particular than others. The devastating impact of Thatcherism upon all sectors of the British economy — private and public services, and manufacturing — is one such noteworthy example. The decline of private services in Denmark, and the relatively slow growth of general public-service employment in the Netherlands point to two opposite roads to mass unemployment. In spite of far above average growth of the labour force in these years, public-service employment in the Netherlands has grown slower than average (1.4 against 1.7 per cent). Italian unemployment has also been favoured by a remarkably slow growth of public services. The very slow growth of private-service employment (as indicated by the relationship between the service totals and the general government figures, which form part of the former) in Germany is also remarkable, particularly if it is taken into account that service employment in Germany, together with Italy, is much lower than in the other major capitalist countries. From Table 30 it further emerges very clearly, that the recently discovered dynamism of the US labour

Table 30
Unemployment and Sectoral Employment Development.[38]

	Service-Sector 1979-83 Annual Growth Per Cent	General Government Annual Growth 1979-82 Per Cent	Manufacturing Index 1983 1980 = 100
Belgium	0.6[a]	1.0	na
Netherlands	3.3[a]	1.4	87
UK	0.4	−0.6	80[b]
Canada	2.1	2.7	87[c]
Denmark	0.1[a]	4.1	na
Italy	2.5	0.8	na
Australia	1.9	1.0	na
USA	1.8	0.5	88
France	1.2	1.2	93
Germany	0.4	1.3	88
Finland	2.7	3.7	na
Austria	2.1	2.0	90
Sweden	1.5	2.4	87
Norway	2.3	3.1	92
Japan	2.1	1.0	102
Switzerland	1.3	1.3	94

a) 1979-82.
b) Second and third quarters of 1983.
c) 1982.

market was a feature of previous decades. In recent years, mediocrity and slow public-sector growth characterize American labour market developments, employment patterns fitting closely together with the medium rate of unemployment of the country.

The low unemployment countries as a group have a better than average short-term employment record with respect to all three sectors: total services employment growth 1.9 per cent per annum, as against an average of 1.6 per cent; 2.0 per cent growth of general government employment (thus excluding nationalized industries) as against 1.7 per cent for our countries as a whole; and a manufacturing employment index of 93, compared with an average of 90. But the intra-group differences are also considerable. Standing out most clearly is Japan, unique in maintaining her manufacturing employment. No general argument about the decisive importance of any one sector for avoiding or reducing unemployment can be sustained. In the current ideological conjuncture, it is the lack of empirical foundation for the anti-public-sector thesis which is remarkable.

The growth of the service sector and the decline of manufacturing is often portrayed as the coming of a *post-industrial society*. But there are nine major ways of entering that society. These may be located along two axes: of unemployment, and private or public services. Both dimensions lend themselves naturally to trichotomization and both have become polarized in the present crisis.

Table 31 in some cases conveys more of the nature of current tendencies than structural features. Britain, France and Italy, for example, still have significant public-service sectors, but their declining importance is striking. In 1970-75, general government accounted for 59.6 per cent of the growth of service employment in Britain and 90.5 per cent in Italy (data for France are lacking). Increasing polarization is indicated by the fact that the US and Japanese public sectors decreased in importance to service-sector growth in 1975-82, from what were already in 1970-75 the smallest contributions, while the heaviest contributions of the early seventies (together with Italy) of Denmark, Sweden and Finland increased further. The prevailing theorizations about the post-industrial society have already become dated and their social

Table 31
Entries into Post-industrial Society.[39]
Contribution of general government to service employment growth 1975-81. Per cent.

Unemployment	Services Growth				
	Private		*Balanced*		*Public*
Mass	UK	7.5	Belgium	54.2[a]	Denmark	104.6
			Netherlands	42.7[a]		
Medium	USA	9.0[a]	Germany	42.4	Finland	105.8
	France	18.5				
	Italy	27.3				
Low	Japan	6.8	Norway	55.2[a]	Sweden	91.5[a]

a) 1975-82.

Table 32
*Profiles of (Un)employment in Descending Rank from
a Labour Point of View.*[40]

	Unemployment	Employment	Employment Growth
Norway	Low	High	High
Sweden	Low	High	Medium
Japan	Low	High	Medium
Austria	Low	Medium	Medium
Switzerland	Low	Medium	Negative
Finland	Medium	High	Medium
USA	Medium	Medium	High
Australia	Medium	Medium	Medium
France	Medium	Medium	Medium
Germany	Medium	Medium	Negative
Denmark	High	High	Negative
Canada	High	Medium	High
Italy	High	Low	Medium
UK	High	Medium	Negative
Netherlands	High	Low	Medium
Belgium	High	Low	Negative

High unemployment = above 10 per cent in 1984, low = less than 5 per cent; high employment = above 70 per cent of population 15-64 in 1983, low = below 60 per cent; high employment growth 1973-85 = growth index above 115. Within identical categories, countries are ranked according to the underlying absolute figures.

myopia is apparent. In this respect they are like their immediate predecessor, the prognosis of convergent industrial societies. The post-industrial society takes on a different meaning according to whether it is being built upon a pool of permanent high unemployment or as a new stage of a full-employment society; and whether a service job is first of all a job in a fast food restaurant and in a business consulting bureau or whether it is in public education and social care.

8. Profiles of (Un)employment

In the final section of this part, we shall put together some of the basic labour market data in profiles of employment and unemployment. As a basis we shall take three key variables, the rate of unemployment, the rate of employment, and employment growth (1973-83). We may group these three-dimensional profiles into a rank order from the point of view of labour. In this perspective, the unemployment rate may be regarded as the most important variable, and the rate of employment as second. We thereby get a yardstick for combining the three dimensions into ranked profiles.

The labour market profiles of Table 32 may also be grouped into six categories, each unemployment category exhibiting a general set and a more specific one.

1. First, there is the *general success story* of Norway, Sweden and Japan.
2. Then there is the more *selective success*, exemplified by Austria and, above all, Switzerland, with medium employment rates and declining or stagnant total employment.
3. *Mediocrity Plus* is exhibited by Finland (high rate of employment) and the USA (high employment growth).
4. *General mediocrity* characterizes Australia and three of the four major countries of Europe (France, Germany, Italy).
5. *Special failures* are Denmark, maintaining a high level of employment, and Canada, with the highest growth of employment in the crisis, both features of exception amid mass unemployment.
6. Finally, there are the *general failures*, the countries of labour market disaster: Britain, Belgium and the Netherlands.

There is, of course, at least one other important aspect of labour market developments, change in real wages.

The exclusivist character of Belgian, French and Italian unemployment is further underlined by the relatively positive development of real wages for employed workers. For Swedish and American workers, 1972-82 was a lost decade. Given the only slightly below average Swedish economic growth record, the poor wage results of the world's strongest trade-union movement are remarkable.

Table 33
Real Wages for Manufacturing Workers 1972-1982.[41]
Hourly earnings for time worked. Index: 1972 = 100

Italy	146	Finland	117
Belgium	143	Switzerland	117
France	143	Canada	116
Austria	133	Denmark	115
Japan	127	UK	106
Netherlands	127	Sweden	101
Germany	122	USA	97
Norway	120		

Wages refer to those of adult men and women. Australian data were not available.

This book's primary task is to explain the diverging rates of unemployment, but an adequate explanation thereof will have to take these more comprehensive labour-market profiles into account. Having made an analytical critique and provided a broad description, let us now turn to the crucial question — why?

III
Politics, Policies, Pressures and Constraints:
Explaining the Economic Politics of Unemployment

1. An Analysis of Differentials

Despite the fact that we found general market relations to be unhelpful in explaining the different impacts that the crisis has had on unemployment in different countries, that is no justification for substituting a 'politicistic' account for an economistic one. Instead of exposing the reader to a new barrage of tabulated tests of other people's theories or untheorized assumptions, this part will be structured along the lines of an alternative explanation.

The approach adopted here is both historical and materialist, taken in a broad and general sense, in terms of an approach to the task of social scientific explanation rather than in terms of specific substantive propositions or of a particular set of concepts. 'Historical' means, above all, two things in this context. First, a concern with time. The patterns of unemployment to be explained have to be located in chronological and social time. Furthermore, current policies and current discourse will have to be assessed in relation to historical traditions of experiences and expectations. Secondly, and more important, a historical approach entails a break with the prevailing mode of explanation in comparative social science research (i.e., the use of measures of co-variation — correlations, regression analysis, etc. — as sufficient explanations). Instead, we will here look for *causal* sequences — trying to trace the paths along which *a* may bring about *b*.

By 'materialist' is meant simply that the effects of values, intentions and policies — for example Keynesian or monetarist — should not be assessed and evaluated on the basis of their intrinsic content alone, but in relation to the pre-given conditions under which they unfold and are deployed. A materialist analysis implies that the impact of, say, political-ideological alignments and of government policies cannot be compared across countries without taking the conditions of each country into systematic account. On this broad and hopefully not very controversial foundation, we will make use of four general notions in developing a differential political economy or — rather, an economic politics — of (un)employment; an analysis directly geared to explaining differential developments and performances. These notions are: politics, policies, pressures and constraints.

Politics has two general connotations here, and each will be analysed with respect to a specific areas of particular relevance in this context. Generally speaking, politics here refers, firstly, to power relations, both in the present and in the interpretation of experiences of the past (which determine political priorities and dominant policy orientations). Secondly, politics will refer to forms of socio-political conflict, conflict regulation and consensus-making. The first is a politics of power, the second is a politics of struggles for power. For our purposes here, there are two political areas of special importance. One is the *politics of full employment*, the location of a commitment to full employment in the power constellation and in the historical experience of a country. The other is the politics of *economic adjustment*, the prevailing forms of conflict and consensus-making within which capital, labour and the government of a given country face the challenges of changed economic circumstances.[1]

The introduction of politics as a major explanatory factor entails, in a historical analysis concerned with causal sequences, that *policies* matter. This has quite rightly been stressed by Fritz Scharpf, who has contributed what is, to my knowledge, the best analytical discussion of the major relevant policy options and dilemmas. Policies do not, however, simply follow from what Scharpf calls 'strategic choice', but are dictated by the history of national political and economic systems.[2]

To analyse and assess policies in a manageable as well as systematic comparative way requires turning the myriad of government measures into a limited set of *policy types* and *policy directions*. Three types of policy appear to be most directly relevant to what we have to explain here: *fiscal policy, monetary policy,* and *labour-market policy.* The last one is often neglected in the Anglo-Saxon discussion, no doubt reflecting its actual underdevelopment in those countries.[3] Labour-market policy is a post-war Swedish invention, promoted by the trade-union economists Gösta Rehn and Rudolf Meidner, and exported to other countries in the late 1960s, when Rehn held a senior position in the OECD Secretariat.[4] The main comparative research on labour-market policy has been developed at the International Institute of Management–Labour Market Policy, at the Science Centre in West Berlin, under the inspiring directorship (up to August 1984) of Fritz Scharpf.[5] Without a systematization of policies, descriptive studies remain analytically inconclusive, thereby allowing any kind of ideological assertion to be made.[6]

With regard to policy direction, a basic classification of fiscal policy is simple. We may divide the latter into expansionist or restrictive. Expansionist means increased government deficit spending together with Keynesian demand-boosting policies — restrictive means the opposite. Under the heading of monetary policy two sub-types may be distinguished: policies regulating the money supply and the accessibility of credit on the one hand, and currency policy on the other. A 'tight' monetary policy means restricting the money supply through high interest rates, credit restrictions etc. (the opposite is usually called 'loose'). 'Monetarism' entails a restrictive fiscal policy and a tight monetary policy, both geared to limiting the supply of money with the aim, first of all, of bringing down inflation and keeping it low. Currency policies are usually classified as 'hard' or 'weak'; a hard currency policy involves either raising the value of one's currency in relation to foreign currencies (revaluation) or keeping it stable in the face of downward pressures and/or foreign devaluations.

The language of labour-market policies is less standardized. The Rehn-Meidner kind is often referred to as 'active', but a comparative analysis will need a broader set of basic options than active and passive. It seems more appropriate for our purposes here to distinguish between *preventive, restrictive and compensatory* labour-market policies, each varying in range or degree of 'activity'. All three refer to government interventions bearing directly — without working their way through markets other than labour or credit markets — on the demand for and supply of labour. 'Preventive' policies, then, are policies aimed at preventing (a rise of) unemployment through maintaining/increasing the demand for labour and/or adapting a given level of labour supply to demand, by measures such as furthering labour mobility, opportunities for vocational (re)training, public works, and subsidies of employment. 'Restrictive' policies are geared to limiting the supply of labour, through early retirement, decreasing the supply of foreign labour, discouraging women from entering and/or staying on the labour market, and the reduction of working hours. 'Compensatory' policies, finally, are intended to compensate for unemployment, by unemployment benefits, disability pensions and such like. Obviously, the three kinds of labour-market policy orientations do not exclude each other, but countries differ greatly in the mix and extent of them.

In the first part we saw that *pressures* upon a given rate of unemployment, in the form of labour-force growth and industrial ageing do not in themselves go very far in accounting for variations in the rate of unemployment. However, that does not necessarily mean that they are without effect. On the contrary, we should regard such factors as pressures — instead of as causes — upon the rate of unemployment, pressures of varying strength, which to varying extents may be countered by policy interventions.

The fourth cornerstone of our explanatory framework is made up by *constraints*. Caution is called for here, because policy constraints are not simply given. They are to a great extent politically and ideologically defined by the power relationships which determine policy priorities and which have been left as a legacy from the past — the institutions and the internalized norms and expectations of the state, the economy, and the society. Furthermore, these relations of power vary significantly among advanced capitalist countries — the preoccupations of the first wave of modern neo-Marxism with *the* capitalist state therefore have to be transcended. Many relevant constraints on a full employment policy have already been covered by the idea of the politics of full employment. They should be excluded from consideration in this paragraph, in order to avoid tautology. Thus, our discussion of constraints will be confined to those related to the international economic context of a given country. For the practical purposes of this analysis, that means factors affecting the balance of payments. These are numerous and of widely varying importance in differing countries. They include: the size and elasticity of foreign trade; the significance and the volatility of financial markets; the location of the currency in the international currency system and the size of foreign debt. These constraints which, strangely enough, are not systematically incorporated in Scharpf's analysis should not be regarded so much as barriers determining which policies are and are not possible, but as challenges to the politics of *adjustment*, which may or may not be capable of staving off the impasse of a given policy orientation. Someone trained in the Marxist tradition, like this writer, might call the analytical framework proposed here a historical materialist dialectic of politics and economics. Adherents to other variants of the same tradition, however, may find it an example of positivist empiricism.

2. The Historical Location of Current Unemployment Patterns

The current group of countries suffering from mass unemployment took on this feature quite recently, and although differences in national unemployment rates have grown since 1973, the great leap, separating the sheep from the goats, took place after 1978. Ever since 1967, when OECD standardization of unemployment statistics begin, three countries have constantly had higher unemployment than the OECD average, but only one of these is a member of the current mass-unemployment group — Canada. The other two were the United States and Italy.[7]

By 1973, Belgium, Denmark and the Netherlands had virtually full employment and were all clearly below the OECD unemployment average. Britain had an average level of joblessness. The first shock of the crisis brought the Belgian (in 1976) and the British (in 1975) unemployment rates above the average for the OECD countries under study. But in 1975 and 1976 unemployment was highest in those countries where it had always been high — Canada, the United States and Italy. From 1977 on, Belgium has been among the countries leading the downhill race.

The 1983 group of countries suffering from mass unemployment dates from 1982. The growth of unemployment in Italy tended to level off after 1977, except for a couple of moderate jumps in 1981 and 1983. American rates increased significantly in 1980 and 1982, breaking through the 10 per cent barrier in the last quarter of 1982 and the first quarter of 1983, then receding somewhat.[8] Dutch unemployment took a stride in 1975 and has stayed above the OECD average since 1978, it began to increase dramatically after 1980.

Mass unemployment, in the sense used here — a standardized rate of above 10 per cent — is a phenomenon unknown until the 1980s — if we disregard the depression of the 1930s. The first OECD country to reach that level was Spain, in 1980. But Spain is only a semi-advanced capitalist country. Among the most developed countries, Belgium and Britain — both in 1981 — were the pioneers of labour-market catastrophe, with 11.1 and 10.7 per cent unemployment respectively. The countries with low unemployment in 1983 have enjoyed that position ever since standardized statistics began in 1967. Austria, Norway and Sweden did undergo some strain in 1982-83, with rates rising to above 3 per cent. Switzerland does have international standardization of its unemployment figures, but Swiss rates are universally acknowledged to be very low.

What about the countries in between in 1982-83? We have already mentioned Italy and the USA. If we compare the average rate of unemployment between, on one hand, France, Germany, Australia and Finland and, on the other, the four persistently low unemployment countries for which standardized rates exist, we find the following differentials: 1967 0.3 per cent, 1974 0.3 per cent, 1975 2.5 per cent.

We therefore have two points of significant increase in the curve. One of these was in 1975 — separating today's low unemployment countries from the rest — the second one occurred in 1982 — making Belgium, Britain, Canada, Denmark and Netherlands into countries of mass unemployment.

3. The Governments of Unemployment

Probably the most obvious question to ask about the politics of full employment is whether governments of varied political colour have different records on unemployment. In the historical spirit of our enquiry we can address that question by looking at which governments were in office during the crucial years when some countries began to experience mass unemployment while others did not.

During the first trough of the mid-seventies, there were eight labour and eight bourgeois governments.[9] Three labour and two

Table 34
The Governments of the Crucial Years
(In cases where there was a change of government in the course
of a year, the government in office for most of that year is given.)

	1975	1982
Belgium	Bourgeois	Bourgeois Coalition[a]
Netherlands	Labour Coalition	Bourgeois
UK	Labour	Bourgeois[a]
Canada	Bourgeois	Bourgeois
Denmark	Bourgeois Minority[b]	Labour Minority[a]
Italy	Bourgeois	Bourgeois Coalition
Australia	Labour	Bourgeois
USA	Bourgeois	Bourgeois
France	Bourgeois	Labour
Germany	Labour Coalition	Labour Coalition
Finland	Labour Coalition[c]	Labour Coalition
Austria	Labour	Labour
Sweden	Labour	Bourgeois
Norway	Labour	Bourgeois
Japan	Bourgeois	Bourgeois
Switzerland	Bourgeois Coalition	Bourgeois Coalition

a) 1981, because this is the year of the sharp increase in unemployment.
b) 1974 for the same reason.
c) A government of Social Democrats, supported by the Communist Party, who together had exactly half the parliamentary seats.

bourgeois governments managed to maintain full employment. One could equally well have expected the balance to be the other way around. Thus, *the departure from full employment in the mid-70s had nothing to do with the political colour of the government.* During the second low point, five of the eleven countries with less than full employment experienced mass unemployment. Seven of the eleven had bourgeois and four had labour dominated governments. By statistical probability, two labour administrations should have led their countries into mass joblessness, in fact only one did. On the other hand, in the same period there were eleven bourgeois dominated governments, four of which presided over more or less full employment. Probability theory would have predicted three. We can conclude that *the bourgeois-labour government divide explains nothing of the development of unemployment in the current crisis.*

4. The Dubious Relevance of 'Corporatism'

It is not altogether clear what 'corporatism' really means. It could indicate monopolistic mediation between interests by powerful organizations, or involvement in policy-making by organizations of both capital and labour, institutionalized forms of class collaboration, or something else altogether. The only thing that is non-controversial is that corporatism matters to the world of social science. This much is plain from the fact that the creator of the modern corporatist paradigm, Philippe Schmitter, has been one of the most successful scientific entrepreneurs of recent times.[10] The concept cannot be ignored by a study of the political economy of unemployment, both because it forms the theoretical backbone of Manfred Schmidt's analyses, and also because it plays a more shadowy role in the work of Scharpf.

Philippe Schmitter ranks Austria and Norway first and second on a list of countries, ordered by their degree of corporatism (Australia and Japan are not considered). Both are low unemployment countries. But the third position is shared between Denmark, Finland and Sweden each of which is in a different one of our three unemployment groups. Among the countries of mass unemployment, the Netherlands ranks sixth, Belgium seventh and Britain fourteenth (out of fourteen countries).[11] Looked at from a slightly different angle, Austria and the Netherlands are clearly the countries with the most elaborate institutionalized mechanism for reaching industrial consensus and both have a generally consensus-oriented policy aiming at the involvement of major interest organizations. This is expressed in institutions such as the Parity Commission (Austria) and the Social–Economic Council (Netherlands). As far as unemployment goes however, Austria is at the top of the league and the Netherlands is at the bottom.

In contrast to his corporatist co-thinker Schmitter, Gerhard Lehmbruch has focused on corporatism as a form of policy-making involving interest groups in decisions across a broad range of issues. According to Lehmbruch's most recent formulation, Austria, Sweden, Norway and the Netherlands are characterized by 'strong corporatism', in other words three countries with low and one with mass unemployment. Medium corporatism exists in Belgium, West Germany, Denmark, Finland and (as a borderline case) Switzerland. In unemployment terms we have here two disasters, two medium-unemployment countries, and one success.

Lehmbruch found weak corporatism in the UK and Italy: one a disaster, the other near the middle of our group of high unemployment countries. The USA, Canada and Australia all represent pluralist societies, none of them very successful in fighting unemployment. For some reason, Japan and France are put together, outside the axis on which degrees of corporatism are measured. They are seen as representing 'concertation without labour' — a slightly astonishing characterization of the first years of Mitterrandism. In any case, there is little comparison between the unemployment record of the two countries.[12]

The most systematic study of Western European incomes policies has been done by an independent-minded student of Lehmbruch, Klaus Armingeon;[13] it covers seven of our sixteen countries. In his view, the two with the most persistent record of 'neo-corporatist incomes policies' for the period 1975-82, are Finland — with a series of broad-ranging packages — and Belgium: one country with medium and another with mass unemployment. Denmark, a land with mass unemployment, had the most consistent record of imposing statutory incomes policy. The lowest level of state involvement in incomes policy was in Sweden, a country with a low level of unemployment.[14]

Another gifted former student of Lehmbruch, Roland Czada, has made a different classification of 'neo-corporatist incomes policies' in the 1970s.[15] According to Czada, five countries had such policies for more than half of the 1970s: Austria, Belgium, Finland, Norway and Sweden. Three maintained a low level of unemployment, one a low to medium rate and one experienced mass unemployment. He found an absence of neo-corporatist incomes policy in Australia, Canada, France, Germany, Italy, Japan, Switzerland and the USA. Of these eight, one reached high unemployment, two maintained a low rate, and the rest fell in between.

'Corporatism' may also be viewed from the angle of industrial conflict or collaboration. That is basically the approach of Manfred Schmidt, who differentiates between 'weak corporatism' — indicated by frequent industrial conflict and by an authoritarian imposition of incomes policies — and 'strong corporatism' — indicated by 'social partnership ideologies', co-operation between governments, unions and employers' organizations, and by a low level of industrial conflict.[16] Schmidt classifies all our five low-unemployment countries and those alone as strongly corporatist.

Weak corporatism, by contrast, Schmidt finds in Britain, France, Italy and the USA.[17]

If Schmidt were right, corporatism, at least by his definition, would provide an attractive explanation. However, his criteria are never made crystal clear, and his own application of them is hardly very convincing. A comparison of the Netherlands and Scandinavia throws considerable doubt upon Schmidt's work in this regard. From my own experience of the Netherlands and Sweden it is rather obvious to me that the ideology of social partnership is much weaker in Sweden than in the Netherlands — and is probably weaker than in West Germany. This finds an institutional expression in the fact that Sweden has no official consensus-making body, such as the Dutch Socio-Economic Council and also in the different ways in which recent safety at work legislation has been implemented in the two countries: through consensual bipartite bodies in the Netherlands and through enlarged bargaining rights for the unions at the workplace in Sweden. Norway, it should be added, is a country with a vigorous postwar tradition, firmly applied throughout the 1970s, of legislative incomes policy — hardly in tune with Schmidt's definition of a 'strong corporatism'.

Let us also look at the evidence of industrial conflict in the period 1974-82.[18] We may divide the countries into three main groups. First, a low strike group of those countries where, on average, less than one per cent of the non-agricultural labour force took strike action in each year between 1974 and 1982. In this group we find Switzerland, Norway, the Netherlands, Germany, Austria and Sweden — in other words, four low unemployment countries, one of medium-high and one of mass unemployment. We can also distinguish a high-strike group of three countries which had more than 10 per cent involvement in strikes: Italy, Australia and Finland. These were all in the medium-high unemployment group in 1983. The rest fall in between, with Japan having more industrial conflict than, for instance, Belgium or the USA.

Whatever measure is used, there is a certain tendency for the countries with low levels of unemployment to be overrepresented among the 'corporatist' ones. But none of the conflicting definitions of 'corporatism' have been found, under empirical scrutiny, to provide us with the necessary or sufficient conditions for the maintenance of low employment. Without detracting from the great value of the bold pioneering work by Manfred Schmidt, we can conclude, that corporatism, however conceived, is hardly relevant to an understanding of why some peoples are more unemployed than others.

5. The Political History of Full Employment

In what countries have there been an institutional commitment to full employment as a political priority, a commitment embodied in powerful policy-making institutions and established as the dominant ethic of economic policy? Government commitment to full employment is a postwar phenomenon, and was pioneered by four European countries. Three of these today belong to our group of low unemployment countries, they are Norway, Sweden and Switzerland. Britain, however, now suffers mass unemployment.

It was in Norway, more than in any other country, that full employment was given the top priority in the construction of postwar society. This was expressed in a common programme of the Norwegian political parties, prepared upon the initiative of the Resistance (*Hjemmefronten*), in the last months of the occupation. The title conveys its main thrust: *Work for Everybody (Arbeid for alle)*. The Norwegian Labour Party played a central part in drawing up the programme — the title of which was taken from an immensely powerful electoral slogan of that party in the 1930s — but the three bourgeois parties, together with the Communist Party, also participated and signed the document.[19]

The programme for full employment was originally part of an ambitious project for economic planning, pioneered at the Oslo School of Econometrics and developed by Ragnar Frisch. But the planning mechanism was gradually diminished or dismantled, and — according to a very well-informed Norwegian observer — planning and forecasting was, by the mid-1950s, less technically sophisticated and developed than its Dutch equivalent.[20] Policy institutionalization of the commitment to full employment was not limited to econometric national budgeting and Keynesian demand management. It also included institutions for special intervention, in the form of vocational training, cheap loans and subsidies for private businesses, and strong efforts in support of regional development plans. For these purposes, an Unemployment Insurance Intervention Fund (*Arbeidsløshetstrygdens Tiltaksfond*) was set up in 1947, followed in 1956 by an Unemployment Insurance Regional Development Fund (*Tybyggningsfond*). When unemployment rose in January 1958 to 2.5 per cent, the Norwegian parliament unanimously voted an additional grant for extraordinary public works.[21]

A major part of the commitment to full employment in Norway has been carried out through direct public subsidies to private enterprise, in the first place to agriculture and to peripherally located small businesses. In 1965, during the postwar boom and well before oil and gas had begun to transform the Norwegian economy — public subsidies to private enterprise amounted to four and a half per cent of GDP. That figure may be compared with similar statistics for the advanced capitalist countries with a comparable level of subsidy to Norway before 1965: Belgium 2.3 per Austria and France 2.2 per cent; Britain 1.6 per cent; Sweden 1.4 per cent; Germany and Italy 1.3 per cent.[22]

Originally, public commitment to full employment in Sweden enjoyed less of a consensus than in Norway. It was promoted by the governing Social Democracy and by the trade unions. In the 1944 'Post-war Programme of the Labour Movement', put out jointly by the Social Democratic Party and the manual workers trade-union confederation (LO), full employment was seen as the first priority.[23]

The programme opens in the following way: 'The whole people at work is the primary goal of our economic policy. Monetary system and public finance, price policy and wage policy, private and public enterprise — everything shall serve the provision of full employment to labour force and the material means of production'. During the long reign of Swedish Social Democracy, that programmatic statement became an institutionalized norm of the Swedish political system, a yardstick against which the suitability of this or that policy undertaking was measured.

In its more concrete manifestations, two aspects in particular of the Swedish commitment to full employment are worthy of note. One is its concentration on the investment side of Keynesian-type demand management. Ever since the Swedish Social Democrats began to develop Keynesian economic policies in the 1930s, the orientation has been much more to counter-cyclical increases of public investment and public works, than to boosting public consumption. In the postwar period, public or publicly planned housing has been a major instrument for this. Thus, to meet the recession of the late 1950s, housing construction in 1959 increased almost 15 per cent above the 1958 level.[24]

Secondly, and much more unique to Sweden, is the emphasis on direct intervention in the labour market *except* on the question of pay. These interventions — termed 'labour-market policy' — entail vocational (re)training, measures to encourage and subsidize labour mobility, subsidized employment of weaker groups on the labour market, and counter-cyclical special public works. They are organized by a very powerful administrative agency, the Labour Market Board, which also runs the local labour exchanges. The Labour Market Board dates back to an ad hoc crisis agency, set up in 1914 for the administration of public works. It was refounded in 1947 and began to expand enormously from the recession of 1958-59 onwards.

The active labour-market policy, like the institution which administered it, could draw upon a pre-war tradition, rooted in an agrarian work ethic. Unemployment policy discussion in Sweden before the Second World War, and in particular before the advent of Social Democratic government in 1932, made a basic distinction between the 'cash line' and the 'work line'. The former referred to unemployment assistance and was unanimously seen only as a secondary measure and a last resort. The latter referred to public works, and was universally regarded as morally superior and as a political priority.[25]

The novelty of the active labour-market policy lay first of all in its explicit formulation and establishment of a public policy mechanism for direct intervention onto the labour market with a view to maintaining full employment, which at the same time left it to the unions to determine the level and the structure of wages by a process of collective bargaining that was formally free. That such an arrangement was formulated by the trade-union movement and not by the government, should not come as a surprise. The Swedish trade unions — in contrast to their Norwegian, British or Dutch counterparts, which all participated in comprehensive efforts at postwar planning and national economic management — had their own economic expertise, as well as the self-confidence of a strong, centralized and in all respects resourceful movement. Even so, it took about a decade before the proposals of Gösta

Rehn and Rudolf Meidner, then fairly junior economists, were accepted, in the late 1950s by the Social Democratic Ministers of Finance.[26] Labour-market policy became a Swedish speciality without comparison anywhere else. When the OECD put together an overview of 'government expenditure on manpower programmes' at the end of the 1960s, Sweden was found to be devoting 1.2 per cent of GNP to such programmes, compared with 0.4 per cent for Canada, Germany and Japan, 0.3 per cent for Belgium, Norway, the UK and the USA and 0.2 per cent cent for Denmark.[27]

The UN Economic Commission for Europe, stationed in Geneva, was sceptical about the maintenance of full employment in Switzerland in its 1949 survey. While Switzerland did have full employment, Gunnar Myrdal and his associates put the country in a group — together with France and the Netherlands — where the 'maintenance (of full employment) may be regarded as more precarious'.[28] No reason for such a conclusion was offered, and the available evidence points in the opposite direction. For example, while industrial employment in Switzerland fell by about eight per cent in 1949, unemployment rose by only a few thousand.[29] That should be interpreted as a strong commitment to full employment in the face of adverse pressure. The way unemployment was prevented in Switzerland should, however, be remarked upon. As the UN survey noticed, domestic full employment was maintained by the export of foreign workers, and with them unemployment. Since the construction of the big tunnels through the Alps at the turn of the century, Switzerland has been significantly dependent on the import of labour, mainly from Italy.[30] On the other hand, this does not correspond to the Marxist idea of an industrial reserve army. On the contrary, it is a policy that keeps the domestic labour market continually restricted, with full employment.

Switzerland is nowadays renowned mainly for its orthodox liberal economics, but the actual record is much more varied. Switzerland was one of the first countries on the European continent to adopt a set of consciously counter-cyclical policy measures. Thus in 1951, a federal law of counter-cyclical taxation was passed (*Bundesgesetz über die Bildung von Arbeitsbeschaffungsreserven*), followed in 1954 by a counter-cyclical public investment law (*Bundesgesetz über die Vorbereitung der Krisenbekämpfung und*

Arbeitsbeschaffung). A bill with the explicit goal of maintaining 'the farmers' estate' was also adopted in 1952.[31] The contribution of these measures to the maintenance of full employment was certainly a minor one in comparison with that of immigration policy, but they do indicate an overall commitment to full employment. An explicit restriction of the full employment commitment to native workers was adopted officially in 1964.[32] The context was not an impending recession, however, but a potentially 'overheated' boom, and formed part of a general policy of protecting the country from the vicissitudes of the world economy, a policy that also included stricter control of incoming capital and temporary controls on the construction of housing.[33]

To look at Britain is to look at failure. The original auspices were promising, however. Full employment was set as a basic political goal in the famous and influential Beveridge Report of 1942.[34] The meaning of high or full employment was originally extremely modest. Keynes apparently did not believe that unemployment could be pushed down below six per cent. When Beveridge in his 1942 report argued for the abolition of mass unemployment, he was thinking of bringing peacetime unemployment down to about 8.5 per cent, a figure that was also mentioned in an appendix to the 1944 government White Paper on Employment, though no official target was set. (Beveridge himself had by then come to the belief that three per cent unemployment might be achievable.)[35]

The British Labour Party Conference of 1944 adopted full employment as a major aim. Labour Party employment policy was largely based on preparing a number of public investment projects, to be put into action at a downturn of the business cycle, but Britain in 1945-51 faced other problems, and the policy was never institutionalized.[36] Any idea of a public labour-market policy was also absent, as emerges from the argument used by Chancellor of the Exchequer Stafford Cripps in the 1948 official economic survey. He suggested that the problem of labour mobility could only be resolved by increasing unemployment by one half.[37] When, after 1951, the Conservatives set out to prove that full employment was safe in their hands, the only major policy thought to be available was general fiscal stimulation.

In one sense, the condition for an active counter-cyclical policy in Britain were quite favourable. Institutional and normative restrictions on government budgetary action attuned to macroeconomic demands did not exist, which was not the case in all countries. Britain also had by then a considerable experience in macroeconomic forecasting and management. Yet, during the 1955-65 period Britain was unique in Western Europe in *destabilizing* her economy through the budget.[38] That is, stop-go policies of deflation and reflation aggravated the swings of the business cycle, most immediately through mis-timing and over-reaction. Underlying the problems was the failure to come to terms with Britain's long-term balance of payment problems. Or, to put it more bluntly, the incapacity of British governments to face up to, and adapt to, Britain's irreversible loss of the status of a first-rank economic power.[39]

The time when full employment ceased to be a primary goal of British economic policy can be located rather precisely in 1966-67, under the second Wilson government.[40] The Tories had resorted to deliberate deflation in 1961, raising unemployment in 1963 and 1964, but this was then followed by a massive reflation, after a change of Chancellor of the Exchequer.[41] The deflation of 1966-67, coming after a vain attempt by the Wilson government to maintain the position of the pound, meant an abandonment of a commitment to full employment by the Labour Party. Only the Netherlands, then under a government composed exclusively of bourgeois parties, had a higher increase in unemployment than Labour-governed Britain in 1967.[42]

Wilson himself has sought to convey a picture of international banking pressure and unjust Conservative criticism, but hardly shows concern over the rise of unemployment.[43] Richard Crossman, a Cabinet Minister and an old political associate of Wilson, wrote in his diary about the April 1967 budget, drawn up by James Callaghan: 'My reflections on hearing that budget were that the Chancellor had deliberately used the occasion to promulgate his new doctrine that we should abandon an artificial prices and incomes policy and revert to a higher rate of unemployment and higher cuts in public expenditure.'[44]

The abandonment of full employment by the Labour Party also laid the basis for the secular decline of the party, which first became visible in 1968.[45] Britain had thus left the club of countries with an institutional commitment to full employment well before the current crisis. Before it became the laboratory of monetarism,

Britain had become the native ground of the Philips Curve, with its full focus on the alleged trade-offs between inflation and unemployment.

Norway, Sweden and Switzerland form a group apart in their strong and continuous postwar commitment to full employment. The Swiss in particular were remarkable; from 1950 to 1974 they ran their economy without unemployment and until 1960 with a rate of inflation lower than in any other country. After 1960 inflation did appear in Switzerland, but only to the extent that by 1974 only Germany, the USA, Canada and Belgium had a lower increase in the household price index than Switzerland. West Germany then had an index figure (1950=100) of 199.6; the USA 204.8; Switzerland 217.2; the Netherlands had 274.3; Sweden 315.6; Norway 325.2; the US 328.7; France 352.1; and Japan 399.9.[46] The truths of standard economics only hold under certain given socio-political conditions.

Austria also has an extraordinary record of commitment to full employment. An international OECD team of 'examiners' wrote on the basis of visits to Austria in 1978, 1979 and 1980: 'Repeated reference has been made to the importance of full employment for the whole social system of Austria. This behaviour, bearing the imprint of the nationalized and other non-private sectors of the economy, like a sort of unwritten law, has clearly had repercussions on all sectors of the economy.'[47] This commitment is, however, of much more recent date than in the three other countries. Stable low unemployment was not achieved until the 1960s.[48] Other preoccupations rather naturally took first place in early postwar Austria: democratic reconciliation between the Social Democratic and the Catholic camps which were virtually at war in the 1930s; the re-establishment of national sovereignty and recognized neutrality — only achieved with the treaty of 1955 — and economic reconstruction and modernization. The specifically Austrian institutions of political economy have their roots in a decision to break with the disastrous past — the impoverished and permanently unstable First Republic, which was first replaced by a clerical Austro-Fascist dictatorship, then swallowed up by Nazi Germany.

Austria has the largest and most comprehensive publicly owned business sector of all developed capitalist countries. By an unanimous parliamentary vote immediately right after the Second World War, the major banks and the major parts of the steel, mining, engineering and chemical industries were nationalized. This measure was carried out as a result of fear that the Allied occupiers would dismantle and remove a large part of Austrian industry, much of which had come into German hands during the *Anschluss*.[49] More than a quarter of manufacturing employment is in the public domain, and two-thirds of the fifty largest companies are state owned.[50] More than twenty per cent of employees in the business sector are publicly employed.[51]

The second particularly Austrian institution of relevance here is the 'social partnership', a set of formal and informal arrangements for comprehensive, centralized bargaining and consensus formation between business and the trade unions. Most important of these is the Joint Commission, which directs wage policy *and* prices, and which also has a major influence on general economic policy.[52] Unions and business are also officially represented on the board of the Austrian National Bank. It should be pointed out that this Austrian 'corporatism' differs significantly from the Dutch variety, above all in the relative strength of labour and capital. Austrian unions are united in one single confederation — while the Dutch trade-union movement is ideologically and functionally divided. The Austrian unions organize about twenty per cent more of the work force than do their Dutch counterparts.[53] And while Austrian business is overwhelmingly small-scale, Dutch economics and politics are overshadowed by the giant multinationals Shell, Philips, Unilever and Akzo. The Austrian unions are also flanked by a big Social Democratic party, capable of forming a majority government on its own, something which prevailing opinion in the Dutch Labour Party seems to think of as an impossible dream.

The commitment to full employment had not been strongly tested before the post-1974 crisis. It was inbuilt into the 'social partnership' institutions, thanks to the strength of labour. That the institutions would survive a degree of political polarization became clear in the late 1960s, when the postwar coalition broke up, and the Catholic ÖVP formed a government of its own. The Joint Commission continued as before, only with more independence from the government. In spite of his right-wing inclinations, the new Chancellor Klaus met the recession with expansionary policies and also introduced a modest Swedish-type labour-market policy

(*Arbeitsmarktsförderungsgesetz*) in December 1968. Industry remained as public as before.[54] The institutions in which the later very visible and audible commitment to full employment were embodied, were a public-cum-private investment oriented 'Austro-Keynesianism' together with an all-encompassing centralized and 'corporatist' incomes policy.[55]

Finally, to see how those countries that were committed to full employment before the crisis correspond to our list of low unemployment countries in 1983-84, we should ask how Japan fits in. We can indeed say that Japan did have an anti-unemployment commitment before the crisis. This is for three reasons. One is the famous big business ethic of 'life-time employment'. This seems to have a background similar to practices operated by large and profitable continental European companies before the First World War and by a few US corporations today, as a means to stave off trade unions and to create a loyal and stable labour force.[56] The differences are, however, crucial. First there is the public, though informal, institutionalized character of the practice, which makes the practice more than just an option subject to the whims of the executives of a profitable corporation. Norms of employment were established in the early 1950s by the Labour Subcommittee of the Industrial Rationalization Council, a bipartite body of government officials and businessmen.[57] The second crucial difference is in the sheer numbers of those protected — about a third more of private employees in the mid-1970s.[58] Another reason why Japan, in her own special way, seems to belong to the group of countries committed to full employment is the situation of the remaining two-thirds of private employees. They have had a long postwar history of full employment. Between 1950 and 1974, Japanese unemployment never exceeded 2.5 per cent per annum.[59] There is certainly a 'dual economy' as far as wages and conditions are concerned, but not with respect to job opportunities. And, as we saw in Part Two, the Japanese rate of employment is relatively high. Japan's high growth record has not yet put her commitment to full employment to a strong test, but conservative governments are certainly not inhibited from active economic intervention by any liberal market or 'deregulation' principles. The stunning economic growth and export performance of Japan has been brought about through 'administrative guidance ... on a much larger scale than anything we know in Europe, let alone in the United States'.[60]

An OECD study carried out before the current crisis was impressed by the full employment policies of the Japanese. Restrictive economic policies in 1962 and 1965, due to balance of payments difficulties, led to 'practically no change in registered unemployment', although some people (women?) were driven off the labour market. Later on, we shall look into the policies deployed by Japanese government and business to deal with the crisis. They show that the maintenance of full employment in the face of the international situation was not simply due to market strength.

6. Bases and Institutions of Full Employment Politics

Of our sixteen countries, we find that only in Austria, Japan, Norway, Sweden and Switzerland was commitment to full employment institutionalized before the onset of the crisis. These commitments were rooted in different historical experiences and had different political justifications. These experiences and motivations may be ranked on a class-based social scale.

The Swedish commitment was, above all, a working-class commitment, the possibility of which was foreseen in wartime full employment. The Norwegian commitment also had a strong labour character to it, but with two qualifications. Firstly, there was a broad political consensus around it from the very beginning, which emerged from a common experience of Fascist occupation and repression; secondly, there was a populist orientation towards maintaining peripheral employment. The Austrian engagement also had a strong working-class basis, but here the traumatic experience of the conflict between the Socialist working class on the one hand, and Catholic farmers and the petit-bourgeoisie on the other — which contributed to the downfall of Austria in the thirties — played a central part. Full employment became part of an effort to preserve social unity and stability, in order to preserve national independence. The Swiss labour movement has always been relegated to a minor position in Swiss society and politics, and in Switzerland full employment became first of all part of a bourgeois programme for the maintenance of general social and economic stability. Stable full employment, stable prices, and stable currency became basic postwar policy goals in Switzerland. The country's international location and the skills of its administrators made these goals compatible with each other. The Japanese commitment developed as part of a national effort at international competition and part of its objective was to prevent working-class independence. The originators of this programme were big capital and the servants of a transformed late-feudal state, in a joint effort linking paternal capitalism with state nationalism.[61]

We may summarize the justification for full employment policies as being based on either one or a combination of two major concerns: the wish of *strong labour movements for full employment* as a class interest and the concern of *certain bourgeoisies for social stability.* In none of our five countries was the institutionalization of the commitment limited to an endorsement of Keynesian demand-management. All have developed a range of specific state interventionist policies. These have included import licensing, credit direction and labour-policy promotion in Japan; control of the supply of immigrant labour in Switzerland; comprehensive 'corporatist' incomes policies and public investment and employment policies in Austria; direct intervention to influence the supply and demand of labour in Sweden; and extensive subsidies to peripheral private enterprise in Norway. In no other countries has the state such a direct impact upon business and employment as in these five — the countries that have succeeded in avoiding serious unemployment during the present crisis.

7. The Politics of Irresolution

The difference between the group of countries treated in section 5 and the rest was *not* over whether full employment was an important political goal at the onset of the crisis. On the contrary, it would be right to say that full employment was everywhere recognized as a central task of macroeconomic management by 1970. The point is rather, that in those five countries full employment was a commitment that had been *institutionalized*; had been embodied in a wide-ranging set of politico-economic institutions and had become part of the 'common sense' of politicians, voters, trade unionists, and businessmen. As we shall see, this institutionalized commitment was crucial, not only in the sense that it led to greater efforts to maintain full employment against the crisis, but also because it significantly increased the chances of such efforts being successful, as a result of the deeply-held expectations of both business and workers.

In most countries, either the official adoption of full employment as a goal of policy came late in the postwar period or it was never put at the centre of the economic institutions of the nation. The fate of attempts to establish full employment as a political commitment in the Anglo-Saxon countries by the end of the Second World War, has been succinctly described by Nixon Apple. In the USA Senator Murray's 1945 Full Employment Bill became the Employment Act of 1946. The original ambition to ensure the 'right to useful, remunerative, regular and full-time employment' turned into the 'responsibility of the federal government ... to promote free competitive enterprise under which there will be afforded useful employment for those able, willing and seeking to work, and to promote maximum employment, production and purchasing power.' The Canadian White Paper on Employment and Income (1945), committed the government to 'a high and stable level of employment'. But this was seen mainly as a matter of promoting private enterprise, and the paper took pains to emphasize what was not needed from the Canadian government's point of view: 'The post-war employment problem is not to be solved by huge expenditures on public works ... The problem of the transition is to maintain the level of employment while substituting private for a large part of public expenditure.' It should, perhaps, be noticed that while the formulation quoted refers most immediately to the transition from a war to a peace economy, it is clear that the Canadian bourgeois government was against any particular institutionalization of employment policies. The Australian Labour government, by contrast, did emphasize the need for institutionalization. This would have involved greater Federal powers of macroeconomic management, a planning apparatus, a norm of counter-cyclical deficit spending and nationalization of the banks. All these proposals were defeated, however, in a series of political battles between 1944 and 1949, when the Labour Party was ousted from office. All that emerged in the end was a vague declaration of intent.[62]

Even during the boom years, what was full employment to official America was fairly high unemployment by the European standards of the time. The 'Economic Report of the President' for

1956 stated that 'The Nation had practically reached full employment' at the end of 1955, when the unemployment rate given in the report itself was 3.6 per cent, and should have been — according to the definition later used by the Kennedy Adminstration — 4.2 per cent. The Kennedy government, in the 1962 'Economic Report of the President' defined the full employment target as 4 per cent unemployment.[63] Canada was a fairly stable high-unemployment country before the onset of the crisis. In the 1960s a more active, supply-oriented labour-market policy was introduced, concerned above all with training of the workforce. But only in the 1970s were more energetic employment schemes developed.[64] Australia, on the other hand, had more or less full employment untl 1975, the result of a resourceful and vigorous economy. When the crisis arrived, there were no institutions in place for combating rising unemployment.[65]

France entered the postwar world with experiences and concerns which, as far as employment was concerned, were largely different from those of other countries. Recorded unemployment in the 1930s was quite low, largely due to its absorption by the rural family-based economy and to the repatriation of foreign, mainly Polish, workers.[66] Jean Monnet and the French postwar planners did not see the threat of unemployment as a problem, but rather foresaw a shortage of labour. It was therefore considered necessary to import one to one-and-a-half million foreign (including colonial) workers over a five year period.[67] French unemployment remained low throughout the postwar period until the crisis of the mid-seventies. That also, however, had the consequence that no powerful institutions for maintaining full employment in times of adversity had been developed. French planning, the object of much international praise in the last decade of the boom, was mainly geared to medium-term growth targets — particularly by means of selective public credit regulation. Counter-cyclical economic management was weakly developed, to put it mildly. The discretionary measures of French fiscal policy were, in fact, strongly pro-cyclical and therefore had a destabilizing effect in the 1958-65 period.

West Germany was long under the influence of pre-Keynesian economics. Referring to the late 1940s and early 1950s, Andrew Shonfield wrote, 'the new objective of full employment on a permanent basis ... hardly figured at all in Germany'.[68] In the 1950s, the Federal Republic probably had the most archaic conception of economic policy of any Western government; this was symbolized in the deflationary accumulation of tax revenue, the so-called *Juliusturm*, developed in order to rearm without the tax-payers noticing it.[69] Only with the 'Grand Coalition' of Christian and Social Democrats, under the then Social-Democratic Minister of the Economy, Karl Schiller, did West German economic policy enter into the modern world, a step enshrined in the Stabilization Act of 1967.[70] The West Germans drew a different conclusion from the inter-war period than the Austrians did. While unemployment was left to care for itself, at least until the vague Work Promotion Act of 1969, the fight against inflation was inscribed in the constitution of the Federal Bank, invested with the independent power and responsibility to preserve the value of the currency.[71] A crude way of putting it, would to be say that the dominant political forces of the Federal Republic of Germany were more concerned with avoiding the ruin of the saving middle classes — which occurred in the galloping inflation of the early twenties — than with preventing mass unemployment — which opened the road to power for the Nazis in the thirties. The fatal role of the *Bundesbank* and of its restrictive monetary policy in the current crisis has been strongly stressed by Scharpf.

In spite of her postwar constitution, stating that the country was to be a republic 'based on labour', the ruling forces of Italy have never cared very much about unemployment. By 1951 the UN Economic Commission for Europe pointed out that Italian government policies were aggravating unemployment.[72] Italy was already notorious for its high rates of unemployment before the onset of the crisis — it achieved its lowest figures in the first half of the 1960s.[73]

In the 1960s and early 1970s Belgium belonged to the group of countries that enjoyed full employment. But this did not issue in any institutionalization of full employment as a policy. The most telling evidence is perhaps the central tripartite negotiations and agreements between employers, trade unions and government, which have taken place on numerous occasions in the postwar period. A number of topics have been dealt with — not only wages but also social and economic policy, broadly taken — but the issue of employment never appeared in the records of these negotiations until 1973. Even then, the words 'full employment' do not occur, even as a goal to be pursued.[74]

The case of Finland is more complex. The 1956 Employment

Act established equilibrium between demand and supply for labour as a policy goal. The main policy instrument resorted to was state and municipal relief works — these were developed to a unique extent in the late 1950s, comprising 4.2 per cent of the adult population in 1958-59.[75] However, these public works seem to have had more to do with a work ethic of, perhaps, Lutheran and 'national reconstruction' origin, than with modern macro-economic management. Keynesian-type macroeconomics spread to Finland only in the late fifties, and more sophisticated state intervention into the market economy dates only from the late 1960s, accompanying broad incomes policy packages.[76] An OECD review team of the mid-70s was unimpressed. It pointed to unsuccessful macroeconomic policies, and the lack of re-training. Some of the arguments, in spite of the team's inclusion of the powerful head of Sweden's labour market board, Bertil Olsson, went in favour of allowing unemployment to increase at the same time as ensuring better compensation through unemployment insurance.[77]

More relevant here, is the fact that the Finnish relief works have been on the decline since the mid-sixties with hardly any variation to take account of the business cycle. Finland was also a semi-developed country, with a large rapidly-declining agrarian sector. Of our sixteen countries, Finland is, together with Italy, the only country that has experienced significant postwar emigration. In the Finnish case, this was mainly to Sweden. Emigration peaked in 1969 and 1970, when the Finnish population decreased by 4.1 and 3.05 per thousand, respectively. But with rising unemployment in Sweden, a net re-immigration occurred in the years from 1971-74 and again in 1981.[78] By international standards, Finnish labour-market policy is still very active, but today's unemployment rate is much higher than in the late 1950s. According to one evaluation, only 2.8 per cent of the workforce were saved from unemployment as a consequence of government policy.[79] The evidence is unclear, however, as another Nordic study has given a figure of 6 per cent employed as a result of special labour-market measures in Finland in 1979 and 1980.[80]

Before the Second World War Denmark was the model country of Nordic progressivism, a pioneer of farmers' education and co-operation, of the labour movement, of social policy and of Social Democratic governments. But with the war things changed. The uniquely subtle form of Nazi occupation kept the Social Democrats in office between 1940 and 1943, and although they never capitulated to the same extent as de Man in Belgium, they emerged from the war partly discredited. Of all our countries under review, Denmark was the only one which had a government clearly to the right of the pre-war regime in 1945-47 — a bourgeois coalition. (The strong advance of the Communists could not compensate for the heavy losses suffered by Social Democracy.) Even in the post-war programme of Danish Social Democracy, full employment was not given the same priority as in Norway and Sweden.[81] Relatively high unemployment plagued Denmark until the 1960s.[82] Social Democratic government policies never went beyond fiscal boosting, construction promotion and, to stop inflationary surges, incomes policies.[83] No overall commitment to full employment took concrete form, and unemployment remained a problem to be confronted, if at all, by social security and unemployment insurance. The OECD review team, writing about Denmark just before the crisis began, were openly sarcastic about the lack of an adequate manpower policy in Denmark.[84]

A relatively ambitious project of postwar economic planning was developed in the Netherlands, although the bourgeois parties limited the power of the new Central Plan Bureau from the start. The main focus of planning then became state planning of wages, a system fully in force until 1963-64, and applied more intermittently thereafter.[85] Full employment was achieved by the mid-1950s, and the Dutch labour market remained tight until 1975. Postwar Netherlands also developed a broad system of socio-political consensus, both in parliamentary politics and industrial relations. The core of the former was the co-operation and coalition of the two biggest parties — the Catholics and the Social Democrats (the Labour Party). These labour-market parties became known in Holland as 'the social partners' — meeting in the tripartite Socio-Economic Council. A type of middle road between the Swiss and Austrian conceptions of full employment ensued, a position boosted by the success enjoyed in employment from 1955 to 1975.

In fact, however, the Dutch system of political economy never became unreservedly committed to full employment. We can only suggest an explanation for this by means of an interpretative hypothesis. As we pointed out above, in comparison with Austria, Dutch labour has remained weak — usually only a junior partner in political and labour-market contexts. In spite of the disastrous deflationary policies of Colijn — the Calvinist ex-manager of Shell — the 1930s were no national trauma for the Dutch. In this respect the Netherlands resembles Switzerland. But unlike Switzerland, religion and with it, secular moralizing, has had a deep impact on the Netherlands. Stability in the Netherlands was not therefore defined primarily in economic terms, but more in terms of institutions of consensus. It is also clear from more recent developments that another current of thought has been operating, though it was submerged until now: that is, a religiously fuelled indifference to paid work. This seems to have originated among Catholics but has remained uncontested by Calvinists. The confessionally-based concern with keeping women at home and the religious evaluation of charity — now broadened to include welfare-state benefits — seem to make full employment a secondary 'materialist' concern.[86]

The most progressive government the Netherlands has ever had was the first postwar cabinet, made up of Social Democrats and some individual progressive notables, among them the Prime Minister Schermerhorn. He presented the goals of his cabinet in a radio speech. In his speech he emphasized the importance which the government attached to full employment but suggested no institutional mechanisms for bringing it about. He did, however, talk of the importance of collaborative institutions for avoiding industrial conflict.[87] In other words, full employment was less important than the avoidance of conflict.

There was, however, a certain degree of commitment. Thus, the recession of 1952 brought forth a series of counter-cyclical measures.[88] Nevertheless, the practice of meeting unemployment with specific public works declined drastically after the 1952-53 recession. In 1952 24 per cent of those put out of the normal labour market got jobs on public works, but in the milder recession of 1967 this was true of only 13 per cent.[89] After 1954, wages on these works were no longer set below the market wage for similar jobs.[90] In 1967 the Dutch Socio-Economic Council brought out a memorandum to the government, concerning 'supplementary employment'. In view of the recession the council did support active measures, but it also said that it abstained from declaring 'whether and to what extent a certain level of unemployment can have a certain function and at what rate of unemployment that boundary would be transcended.' It also defined the goal of economic policy as the reaching of 'optimal employment, taking into account the other four goals of socio-economic policy.'[91] In a memorandum of 1969 on labour-market policy, the Council reiterated its objective, of 'optimal employment'.[92] This 'evasive expression' used by the tripartite Dutch organ, without trade union reservations being expressed, may be compared with the equal importance which the Austrian Chambers of Trade and Industry Organizations (*Handelskammerorganization*) attach to 'stability' and 'full employment'.[93]

Conclusion

There can be no doubt that the weight given to the objective of full employment and the political attention it has received, has varied widely in the postwar period. It should also be clear by now that the concern with employment has been particularly great and firmly rooted in Norway, Sweden, Switzerland, Austria and Japan. Britain abandoned that concern in the 1960s, her Labour government being more devoted to the pound than to full employment. In the other countries of the European continent, full employment was a secondary or even a neglected issue. In Australia, Canada and the USA, the commitment was given no precise institutional form, and even when full employment was allotted a concrete meaning, as in the USA, the standards were much lower than they were in Europe. In retrospect, then, we can say that an alert observer of the advanced capitalist countries in 1973-74 should have been able to predict which countries were likely to maintain low unemployment in the future.

The importance of deeply institutionalized practices and expectations is highlighted by the very uneven effectiveness of general, Keynesian-type demand-expansion policies, itself an important reason for the vacillating policies and right-wing turns in the countries where full employment commitments have not been so institutionalized. One way of summarizing this might be to tabulate the kinds of budget policy pursued in the two decisive periods of the crisis hitherto, the mid-seventies and the early eighties. Perhaps the best measure available of this is the general budget balance, cyclically adjusted (that is, disregarding surpluses or deficits due only to changes in the economy and net of interest payments, whose effects on demand are ambiguous). Two countries, which failed to maintain full employment, initially met the crisis with clearly expansionary budget policies: Germany and Denmark. The relatively moderate Swedish expansion, though well above the average was the product of a major boost to the economy in 1974 (+3.4 per cent of potential GDP), followed by contraction in the ensuing years. The Heath government gave the British economy a massive injection in 1973 (+8.5 per cent), just before the crisis, which was aggravated by deflation.

A remarkable phenomenon emerging from Table 35 is that the low unemployment countries all appear to have pursued restrictive budget policies in the 1981-82 recession, Japan and Sweden quite strongly. (Denmark, by contrast, which plunged into mass unemployment, had more budget expansion than most countries in the second period.) These results provide good fuel for controversies among economists. But one reasonable interpretation would be

Table 35
Expansionary and Restrictive Fiscal Policies in the Crisis.[94]
The lower the value, the more expansionary the budget.
Cyclically adjusted budget balances in per cent
of potential GDP/GNP.
Cumulative annual change over the previous year.

	1974-75	*1981-82*
Australia	1.2	0.7
Austria	−0.8	0.3
Belgium	0.9	−0.3
Canada	−2.6	0.5
Denmark	−2.2	−5.0
Finland	−2.2	0.3
France	−0.8	−1.4
Germany	−4.7	1.6
Italy	−2.2	−3.4
Japan	−2.2	1.5
Netherlands	−0.8	−0.4
Norway	−1.7	−1.1
Sweden	−2.4	0
UK	0.4	4.4
USA	−0.9	−0.4
Average	−1.4	−0.2

that the initial response to the crisis was crucial, setting the stage for the impact of later shock waves. In this initial response, an expansionary budget policy was necessary, but not sufficient. Secondly, a good temporal fit between threats to employment and budget response was decisive. Sweden averted a second threat to her full employment in the late 1970s, with massive reflation in 1978 and 1979 (cumulative impact +4.5 per cent), and Japan did the same in 1982 (+3.5 per cent). In 1981, when Danish unemployment rose by two percentage points, on the other hand, Danish budget policy was quite passive (impact 0.0 per cent). By the time of the 1982 reflation, it was too late.

It is at any rate necessary to move beyond the discussion of single policies — e.g., for or against Keynesianism, although the pro-Keynesian argument gets more support from the evidence than the anti-Keynesian one — and take broader institutional complexes, historical traditions and time sequences of contemporary history into account. Historically formed institutions affect the outcomes of economic crises. However, a true historical explanation never stops before the causal sequence has been laid out. Therefore, we must investigate how the politics of full employment and those of irresolution worked themselves out in actual crisis policies under specific given pressures, and how adjustments to policy constraints were carried out in practice.

8. Facing the Crisis: Five Roads to Success

The full story of a decade of crisis management obviously cannot be told here. Instead, we will attempt a systematic overview. First we shall look at pressures on the level of employment, then we will survey what kind of fiscal, monetary, and labour-market policies were pursued. We will note what happened to public-sector employment, and finally we will raise the question of constraints and adjustment to them.

Pressures

The rate of growth of the workforce was slightly lower in the five low unemployment countries during 1972-73 than the OECD average, and somewhat higher than the EEC average (in Sweden it was below the EEC average as well).[95] For the period

1979-82, Austria and Norway had a growth in work force that was above the OECD average. Growth in Japan was above the West European average. Switzerland, after a unique decline of the labour force in 1975-79, experienced average growth, and Sweden only lagged 0.1 per cent behind.[96] The differences were fairly small — except for the policy-induced Swiss decline in the latter half of the 1970s. Among the successful countries, Sweden has had less labour-force pressure on employment than Japan, Norway, and above all, Austria.

For the purposes of this kind of analysis overall economic decline may be regarded as another important pressure upon a given level of employment. In this respect, the group of five, which separated itself from other advanced capitalist countries in 1975, contains the two countries with the most drastic changes of economic growth rates from one year to the next. The Japanese economy went from 8.8 per cent growth in 1973 to a 1 per cent decline in 1974 and the Swiss went from 1.5 per cent growth in 1974 to 7.5 per cent decline in 1975. The other three countries had rather small fluctuations at this time: Sweden an 0.8 per cent swing between 1973 and 1974 — greater between 1976 and 1977 when the figure is 2.7 per cent — Norway 1 per cent between 1974 and 1975, but still with an absolute growth level of 4.2 per cent; Austria had a swing of 4.3 per cent between 1974 and 1975.[97] In 1982, when the other eleven countries of our study divided into groups of medium and mass unemployment, the five countries experienced swings that were on the whole, much smaller. Sweden and Austria then had an increased rate of growth as had the EEC. Japan experienced a 1.2 per cent slowdown in its rate of growth — worse than the OECD and EEC averages, but still remaining at a uniquely high level of growth. After Canada and the USA, Switzerland had the largest negative growth swing between 1981 and 1982 — 2.7 per cent — which together with an economic decline of 1.2 per cent, was the fourth worst record of our sixteen countries in 1982.[98]

To what extent these swings in economic growth rates were due to structural features of the economy and how far they were caused by stabilization policies need not concern us here. But we can conclude that the pressures upon employment in the successful countries were not less than in those which failed. Within our five countries, pressures on employment were weakest in Sweden and strongest in Switzerland and Austria, for different reasons.

Fiscal Policies

All the successful countries met the crisis with expansive
Keynesian fiscal policies, though much less so in Switzerland than
elsewhere.[99] Most surprising, given the conventional wisdom is the
importance of Keynesian demand-management policies in Japan.
As we have seen above, the export dependence of Japan is rather
small in comparison with West European countries and, contrary
to how it may appear to competitors, the Japanese recovery after
the blow of the oil crisis of 1974 was led by increased domestic
demand. Up to three-quarters of Japanese economic growth
between 1975 and 1979 was accounted for by rising domestic
demand. Between 1981 and 1982 the net impact of foreign transactions — including not only trade in goods, but also freights,
travel, licences, etc., on which Japan is running a deficit — was
negative, while domestic demand contributed a growth of 6.2 per
cent.[100] From a surplus of 2 per cent of GDP in 1973, the public
sector went down to a deficit of 4 per cent in 1975, where it
remained until 1982.[101] Public expenditure in Japan was lowest
among our sixteen countries, but between 1973 and 1982 it grew
in absolute terms by more than the OECD and the EEC averages,
from 22.1 to 34.5 per cent of GDP, and in proportional terms faster
than any other country.[102] The balance of current public sector
receipts to total outlays was 0.3 per cent of the Gross Domestic
Product in 1973, going down to a deficit of 3.3 per cent in 1975
and 4.3 per cent in 1982.[103] Apart from its informal but powerful
controls, the Japanese state also has a very important lever over
investment. In 1982, it accounted for 29.4 per cent of total investment (gross fixed asset formation), whereas the Dutch state —
spending almost twice as much relative to the national product,
accounted for only 15.9 per cent of the country's investment.[104]

By contrast, fiscal expansion in Switzerland was extremely
modest. The balance of current government income and expenditure — data on total government outlays are not available for
Switzerland — decreased from 4.6 to 3.4 per cent of GDP between
1973 and 1975, reaching 3.2 per cent, thus still remaining strongly
positive, in 1982.[105] Current government disbursements grew
much more slowly in Switzerland than in other countries, and from
a very low starting-point (from 24.2 per cent of GDP in 1973 to 30
per cent in 1982).[106]

Sweden pursued a vigorously expansive fiscal policy. Between

1973 and 1975, the balance of current public receipts and total public-sector outlays decreased from 3 to −0.2 per cent of GDP, running up to a deficit of 7.6 per cent of GDP in 1982. The Austrian response was even stronger from a balance of 0.6 per cent of GDP in 1973 to a deficit of 3.2 per cent in 1975, but from then on slowing down, ending up with a deficit of 3.6 per cent in 1982. Total government outlays increased in Austria from 41.3 per cent of GDP in 1973 to 50.3 per cent in 1982, after a more restrained growth since 1978, while in Sweden growth continued unabated — in spite of the Social Democrats' loss of office in 1976 — reaching a figure of 67.3 per cent of GDP by September 1982.[107]

The Norwegian fiscal situation is unique, because of the very important oil and gas revenues — both resources exploited mainly by the public corporation Statoil, in stark contrast to the Dutch concessions to Shell and Esso. The use of it has been expansive, though less so than in Austria and Sweden. The balance of current receipts and total outlays of government was 5 per cent of GDP in 1973, going down to 3 per cent in 1975, then up again to 4 per cent in 1982. The development of total public expenditure has been quite restricted — from 44.6 per cent to 48.8 per cent of GDP — indeed the slowest growth of any of our countries.[108] The initial fiscal policy response to crisis was therefore strongest in Austria, closely followed by Japan and Sweden. Deficit spending continued longest in Sweden and, in spite of expansionary changes, never developed in Norway and Switzerland.

Monetary Policy

The importance of monetary policy, as an explanans of high unemployment, has been stressed by Fritz Scharpf in a comparison between Austria and Germany.[109] The evidence is not quite overwhelming. While it is true that Austrian real long-term interest rates became negative (1 per cent) in 1974 — in 1977, 1978 and 1982, they were not only positive but higher than the German ones.[110] Japan and Switzerland had negative long-term interest rates — defined as nominal interest on five years or more government bonds minus the inflation rate — before the crisis (Switzerland −4.4 per cent in 1972 and 2.4 per cent in 1973, Japan −4.2 per cent in 1973). In 1974, the Japanese long-term rate amounted to −9.4 per cent, second only to Finland, whereas Switzerland tightened her monetary policy in 1974-75. After that it returned to more normal patterns, but again rose sharply toward the end of the decade, reaching 5.9 per cent in 1980. Swiss, Norwegian and Swedish interest rates were kept low, diving to −5.3 per cent in Sweden in 1975 and to −4.2 per cent in Norway in 1980.[111]

At the instigation of trade-union economists, Austria opted for a hard currency policy in 1979, revaluing the schilling against the Deutschmark and then tying the former to the latter.[112] The Swiss franc appreciated in value by about sixty per cent between 1973 and 1977.[113] Japanese yen also rose from 1975. By contrast, the Swedish and Norwegian crown depreciated strongly after 1976 and 1977, respectively.[114] With the exception of Switzerland, the level of the money supply has not been an important policy goal for the full employment countries.

Labour-Market Policies

By labour-market policy is meant all kinds of major interventions in the economy that directly affect the demand for and the supply of labour, rather than in general fiscal and monetary policies that act more indirectly. The development of ordinary public employment will be considered separately. Labour-market policy started in Sweden, so let us begin our analysis there. The orientation of Swedish policy changed in the latter half of the 1970s, in two ways. Supply-side labour-market policies, mainly aimed at improving the skills and mobility of the labour force, increased in relative importance from about a quarter of total expenditure in 1973-74, to 38 per cent in 1981-82. Secondly, direct subsidies to private corporations, mainly in shipbuilding and steel, increased strongly, with the aim of preventing redundancies, and thereby to gain time for the restructuring of the branches involved and to provide new job opportunities in the affected areas.[115]

The impact was considerable. Disregarding the effect of subsidies to continue non-profitable production, about 4 per cent of the labour force were kept off the unemployment register by measures of special public works and vocational retraining. Without this active labour-market policy, the Swedish rate of unemployment would have been about 6 per cent in 1978-79, well above that level in 1982, and above 7 per cent in 1983.[116]

The costs of such a policy are not prohibitive; about 3 per cent of GDP in 1978-80 and 1982-83, rising to between 4.1 and 5.1 per cent if we include temporary subsidies, and to 4.6 per cent in 1978-79 and 5.9 per cent in 1982-83, if compensatory unemployment benefits are also taken into account.[117]

Since the measures are limited in duration for any given individual, their long-term failure would become visible in higher rates of unemployment and/or lower rates of employment. Neither is the case, as emerges from the tables in parts one and two of this book. It should be noted that a peak of such labour-market policy efforts occurred under bourgeois political rule. Between September 1976 and September 1982, Sweden was governed by a series of bourgeois governments. This continued commitment to full employment has to be seen as an effect of previous political institutionalization.[118]

The other country where labour-market policies played a decisive role in keeping unemployment low was Switzerland. But here the policy orientation was restrictive, concentrating on limiting the supply of foreign labour. If all foreign workers in Switzerland in 1973 had been allowed to stay, unemployment in Switzerland would have been 7.8 per cent in 1978 — other things being equal. In fact, the rate was 0.4 per cent.[119]

As we noticed in part two, the restrictive Swiss labour supply policies also had effects on women — decreasing female participation in the labour force to an unparalleled degree. This was a quite explicit goal, expressed in the 'Deconstruction Code' (*Abbau-Kodex*) of the Swiss employers' organizations, albeit in the somewhat euphemistic form of a 'second earning marriage partner' (*Zweitverdienende Ehepartner*).[120]

Although figures of comparable accuracy cannot be marshalled, it seems quite clear that the main burden of Norwegian full-employment policy was also carried by special intervention in the labour market. In this case it primarily took the form of direct government subsidies to private enterprise. These subsidies, already uniquely high by 1967 — before the crisis and before the oil revenue — increased from 5.2 per cent of GNP in 1970 to 6.2 per cent in 1975 and then to a peak of 7.7 per cent in 1978. The countries coming closest to this were still far behind: Belgium and Sweden at 4.2 per cent.[121] The importance of this will be appreciated when we look at the findings of a firm of Norwegian business consultants. They found that in 1972 13 per cent of the manufacturing work force were employed in enterprises where the wage bill exceeded the value of production (value added, i.e., before profits and interest); by 1980 this had grown to 16 per cent, corresponding to 3.25 per cent of the labour force.[122] It is not without interest to note that in 1965 and in 1972 — but not in 1980 — Norway had a bourgeois government. Again, the institutionalized commitment to full employment survived a major political change. In addition to subsidies, Norway has a relatively active labour-market policy of a more conventional type. In 1983, such measures seem to have encompassed about 1.5 per cent of the labour force.[123] We may, therefore, safely conclude that without their particular interventions in the labour market, Norway, Sweden and Switzerland would have belonged to the medium unemployment countries. The Austrian and the Japanese cases, however, are more complex.

Restrictive labour-market policies played an important part in Austria in the 1970s. Other things being equal, if the numbers of foreign workers in Austria in 1973 had remained there in 1978, unemployment would have almost doubled — from 2.1 per cent to 4 per cent.[124] The effect of Swedish-type labour-market policies was insignificant — 0.3 per cent of the labour force were kept from unemployment by these methods in the 1970s.[125] Compared to the results of repatriating foreign workers, the effect of the unemployment policy of Austrian public industry was negligible. On the basis of one Austrian comparison of changes in employment patterns in the private and public sectors between 1973 and 1977 — sectors not strictly comparable because of differences in size and branch distribution — we may conclude that the maximum effect of public enterprise was to diminish unemployment in 1977 by 0.2 per cent.[126] As we have seen, in relation to the quite positive development of manufacturing production in Austria, no particular 'labour hoarding' is visible.

The paternalistic labour-market policies of Japan have certainly played a role in keeping Japanese unemployment low, but how much of a role is difficult to ascertain. The growth of employment in Japan after 1973 has been most rapid in the smaller enterprises, with their poor conditions of employment.[127] Structural changes have been considerable in Japanese industry since 1975. Between 1975 and 1980, employment in textiles decreased by 11 per cent, in iron and steel by 16 per cent and in shipbuilding by 37 per cent.[128] The practices of employers varied, but in the steel and the shipbuilding industries very few employees of big corporations were made compulsorily redundant. Redundancy was handled by natural wastage, and by transfer to other, more prosperous, branches of the same conglomerate.[129] Despite robotization and the introduction of microelectronics, big corporations — such as the Nissan motor company and others— have agreed to maintain employment and wages.[130] Given the relations of strength between capital and labour in Japan — heavily balanced against the latter — this must be seen as an expression of a paternalist institutionalization of a commitment to full employment.

The Policy Record

Policies do matter in the face of a worldwide crisis. In Switzerland, supply restrictive labour-market policies reduced unemployment by more than 7 per cent, and promotive supply and demand-side labour-market policies reduced unemployment by 4 per cent. Direct state intervention has also been crucial to Norwegian full employment. Austria and Japan owe their low unemployment to a more complex configuration of policies, the individual effects of which are more difficult to gauge. The public fiscal policy, national bank interest policy, and public and private business employment practices worked closely together in the context of what were, for different reasons, inherently strong economies.

In the light of contemporary comparative political economic historiography, the prevailing debates about Keynesianism versus monetarism; public sector versus private sector; export orientation versus domestic demand all appear jejune, and fuelled more by ideological heat than by scientific knowledge and analysis. Nor is an active labour-market policy reducible to a reduction in working-time with compensation for loss of pay, as the Dutch discussion seems to insist. The five roads to success in the fight against unemployment are all different, and none of them follow one of the major economic recipes. In a sense, that should not be a surprise. According to conventional economic theory, of whatever variant, a global capitalist crisis will lead to mass unemployment. The point is, however, that the same crisis is encountered by different national political systems, with different institutions and different policies. Other things are no longer equal in the world of actually existing advanced capitalism.

Constraints and Adjustments

The countries that have been successful against unemployment are operating under the constraints of international markets and the logic of domestic capitalist enterprise. However, those constraints seem to be less rigid in the successful than in the unsuccessful countries. This is a given, the looser constraints deriving largely from the outcome of politico-economic conflicts and options in the past. The state has more powers vis-à-vis international and national markets than in the other countries. The forms and the usage of these powers, however, vary enormously among the five countries.

None of them is a member of the European Community, and crucial features of the particular anti-crisis policies pursued by each country would have been either outright impossible or extremely difficult to carry out within the EEC (by a single country). The harsh immigration controls and restrictions operated by Austria and Switzerland would not have been possible (at least not to the same extent). A major part of the Norwegian subsidies policy probably would be prohibited in the EEC. The wide-ranging protectionist measures characterizing the Japanese build-up and the until-recently effective insulation of Japan's financial market, would hardly have been possible. The 16 per cent Swedish devaluation in the autumn of 1982, a crucial instrument in a policy of adjustment to constraints, would have been difficult to assert within the EEC.

But it is not only an inherited political capacity to resist market constraints which is remarkable in the countries of success. The oil crisis unleashed feverish activity by the Japanese state as well as by private business (with the two usually working in unison) under the co-ordinating guidance of the former. The famous Ministry of Trade and Industry (MITI) introduced the concept of a 'plan-oriented market economy', and embarked on vast programmes of energy restructuring (away from oil) and conservation. For the downscaling and restructuring of depressed industries — ship-building, textile, basic metals, certain branches of chemical industry — planned cartelization was developed. When national interests were seen as threatened, the Japanese state could also strike out against private business. Thus, in November 1973 officials of the Fair Trade Commission raided the offices of twelve petroleum companies which were suspected of price-rigging.[131]

The export offensive resumed, but Japan's permanent deficit on 'invisible' trade has not prevented deficits on current account from reappearing in 1979 and in 1980. For 1981 and 1982 the Japanese surplus — now restored — was less than half the British one.[132] Expansive demand management also pushed up government deficits to a level of 4.8 per cent of GDP in 1979, only surpassed by Italy and Belgium. The much-vaunted British deficit was limited to 3.2 per cent.[133] In spite of an unprecedented rise in the value of its currency since 1973, Switzerland has been able to maintain a surplus on current account every year except 1980, and trade in manufactures has always kept a positive balance. The growth of the export volume has not been very big over the long-run, but in the 1973-77 period, Swiss exports, and foreign trade as a whole, increased above the average for comparable countries.[134] The industrial modernization behind this impressive performance was orchestrated by private business associations, financially assisted by the state.[135]

In order to maintain national control and stability, the Swiss authorities have attempted to stave off the tendency for the franc to become an international reserve currency. The Swiss have therefore opted for an opposite policy to that of the luckless British, who have tried to retain the special status of the pound without having the economic muscle to do so. But since about 1980, the Swiss have come to accept the status given to their currency by international finance markets.[136] In spite of this, however, the authorities have continued to operate monetary policy and interest rates aimed at domestic stabilization. Interest rates in the 1980s have been kept well below those of other financial centres and long-term real interest rates have been kept close to zero. Institutionalized expectations, based on the Swiss historical record of economic stability, have been strong enough to affect capitalist behaviour on financial markets, thereby greatly easing the international constraints posed by the strong dollar and high American interest rates.[137]

The Norwegians built up their oil industry with huge foreign loans and also used foreign finance to protect full employment in the mid-70s. This led up to a position where its current account deficit with the rest of the world amounted to 14.1 per cent of GDP in 1977. Adjustment came swiftly and effectively, however, involving a restriction of demand and a statutory wage and price freeze in 1978 and 1979.[138] By 1980, current balances with the world were back into the black again. But non-oil exports and manufactures have continued to do poorly, and behind the so far steady walls of North Sea revenue, problems of adjustment seem to be piling up.[139]

The enduring international crisis put Sweden's unemployment resistance policies under severe strain from the end of the 1970s. Export-oriented industry lost a substantial proportion of its market share and manufacturing production declined strongly. Profits in manufacturing dipped lower than in other countries — in 1977 and 1978 much lower than in Britain. Government debts and deficits were piling up, the latter reaching a peak of 6.2 per cent of GDP in 1982. Since 1974 the current balance of transactions with the world was deficitary.[140] A change of government policy was announced in the winter of 1982, involving cuts in social expenditure and marginal tax rates, but that line, presented by the bourgeois government, did not materialize because of the change of government in the September 1982 election.

Instead, a new adjustment programme started with a 16 per cent devaluation of the crown, aimed at boosting international competition — a road already taken with some success by the then bourgeois government in 1981. The unions agreed to co-operate in staving off inflationary pressure by wage moderation. The budget deficit was diminished by a combination of tax increases and expenditure cuts. The commitment to maintaining full employment was backed up with a public investment programme in the transport, energy and constructions sectors. So far (by the end of 1984) this adjustment has been successful. Exports have picked up strongly, helped of course by the general international upturn. The balance of trade has become positive and the total foreign balance has improved considerably. Inflation remains higher than in most Western countries, but has fallen substantially. Low unemployment has been maintained, but is now more secure than before.[141]

The Austrians have been original enough deliberately to increase international constraints on them by linking their currency to the Deutschmark, against which the schilling was revalued in 1979. As a result, Austrian interest rates also had to follow German ones upwards. The justification was control of inflation and legitimation of a strict incomes policy. Inflation has indeed been kept very low in Austria; for the 1971-80 period, only Switzerland and West Germany had a lower rate. In the 1980s, the Japanese have been even more successful in this area, but the

Austrian record remains impressive.[142]

The Austrian economy has maintained a strength throughout the crisis, a strength which is very often neglected in the standard references to incomes policy and public-sector 'labour hoarding'. Thus, for 1973-80, Austria had the fastest growth in exports after Japan — 7.2 per cent annual growth, as compared with Japan's 9.1 per cent and West Germany's 4.3 per cent.[143] The rate of savings and investment has been high in Austria. Though it has fallen off in the crisis, the Austrian rate of savings has kept its lead over the OECD average, and somewhat increased with regard to the rest of Western Europe.[144].

Given this intrinsic economic strength and given the institutionalized incomes policy, an expansive full employment policy was possible without provoking a flight of capital and speculation against the schilling. But external constraints have nevertheless forced adjustments. Fiscal policy was tightened, with deficits annually reduced since 1979.[145] In spite of her excellent export performance Austria has kept her historic foreign trade deficit, partly counteracted by revenues from tourism. The total current balance has often run into deficit, and after a new fall in 1983 (which was aggravated by a capital outflow following new taxation on interest income), a restrictive policy was adopted for 1984. This caused a fall in real consumer purchasing power, which was expected to recover in 1985.[146] Unemployment has been predicted to increase somewhat, but will stay below that of the medium unemployment countries.[147]

In all the successful countries, external constraints have made policies of adjustment necessary. These adjustments have worked so far in all five cases. They have not become part of a stop-go cycle, and they have been brought about without major social divisions and conflicts. It seems meaningless to group the varying modes of adjustment under a common rubric of 'corporatism'. In three of the five, centralized incomes policies have played an important part in the adjustments, but neither in Japan nor in Switzerland was this the case. Both have decentralized forms of wage determination. The forms of incomes policy also vary considerably, from the all-embracing 'Social Partnership' in Austria, to the statutory state interventions in Norway, and the informal co-ordination of labour-market organizations in Sweden, jealously guarding their independence.

The immediate manner in which constraints have been adjusted to has been very different. Switzerland and Sweden form polar opposites in this respect. In the former, an internal reshuffling of the economy took place, which in spite of drastically increasing costs — largely due to currency appreciation — made the capture of new markets possible. Some multinational corporations apart — alone among small countries, Sweden has two profitable car companies — Swedish capital was losing out on the crisis-hit world market. In the debate in Sweden, this is largely attributed to rising labour costs in the mid-seventies, but the Swiss experience shows that it could equally well be regarded as an outcome of managerial failure. To Swedish export business, the new Social Democratic government of 1982 appeared as a saviour, with its 16 per cent devaluation.[148] The subtle Austrian public-sector managers, the keenly modernising Japanese traditionalists, and the new Norwegian oil men successfully manoeuvred between the high-cost Swiss competitors and the devalued low-cost Swedish ones.

Underlying the variations, there seem to be two common important patterns, which are certainly inter-related. One is a remarkable national unity around a set of concrete policy priorities. Full employment is always one of these, but apart from that the content of this national unity varies. Secondly, largely because of this consensus, there appear to be strong expectations by all important economic actors in the successful countries that there will be a fairly long-term continuity in basic government policy orientation. This tends to prevent self-fulfilling prophecies of policy failures and reversals. This credibility of policy measures is thereby enhanced, thus making adjustment measures more effective.

9. Roads to High Unemployment

Sorting out the Failures

We should be clear about what we mean by 'failure'. From a working-class perspective, unemployment is obviously an expression of political and economic failure. This is also true from the perspective of a broad national consensus in Japan,

Switzerland, Sweden, Norway and Austria. Without denying either my socio-political or my national allegiances, I do not here define failure in specific class or national terms. This is mainly due to a methodological principle. I think there is an extremely fruitful creative potential to be tapped by bringing to bear a deliberate tension between political dedication and commitment to scientific objectivity, and between national rootedness and the inter-nationalism of comparative study — Karl Marx and Max Weber have both, in their different ways, taught me that.

The notion of failure is not quite as simple as it seems, because there are important political and theoretical forces for whom a certain amount of unemployment is clearly *not* an indicator of failure — sometimes it may even, *sotto voce*, be regarded as an expression of success. The late-Keynesian notion of an inflation–unemployment trade-off, graphically formulated in the Philips Curve, became widespread just before the crisis. The monetarist economists and ideologues, important tutors of Thatcher and Reagan, accepted this notion of trade-off, at least in the short run, and quite explicitly gave their priority to combating inflation. They implied, and sometimes clearly said, that a rise in unemployment would be part of economic success — i.e., would lead to the lowering of inflation.

Furthermore, in blunt class terms, the bourgeoisie has often seen high unemployment as a means to roll back the power of the working class and trade unions. Such views are not only found in the embattled right-wing camps of Thatcher and Reagan. Thus, in the autumn of 1981, when unemployment was beginning to rise dramatically in the broad-minded, recently secularized Netherlands, academic voices could be heard, declaring: 'A bright spot of our economy ... seems to be that the strong rise in unem-ployment has led to a decline in the willingness of workers to strike and thereby in the power of the trade union leaders.'[149] In order to fully appreciate this professorial wisdom, the reader should know that the Netherlands has a frequency of strikes that is among the lowest in the world, surpassed only by Switzerland and Austria in the developed capitalist world, and that Holland also has some of the most undemanding trade-union leaders. In fact, in their explicit espousal of wage cuts during the crisis they are probably without equal.

Despite all this, persistent mass unemployment is not in the interests of most sectors of capital, and no right-wing government boasts of its record of high unemployment. On the contrary, even the Thatcher government wants to convey the message that it aims to combat current unemployment. In the House of Commons debate on unemployment on 6 December 1984, Chancellor of the Exchequer Nigel Lawson felt the need to express 'a very great worry' about the rate of unemployment which, however, could only be brought down by wage reductions.[150] Reagan has also wanted to stress that his government has reduced unemployment. Even in the calmer post-election atmosphere, Reagan, summarizing his domestic policies, said: 'We started out to reduce the size of Government. We started out to provide the incentives, taxwise, that would create economic growth and reduce unemployment.'[151] Of course, he is not particularly eager to relate that unemployment is still higher in November 1984 than it was in 1980 (although there has been some improvement since 1982).

The annual rate of unemployment in the USA in 1980, when Reagan was first elected, was 7 per cent. In November 1984, after a big boom, it was 7.2 per cent.[152] There does, therefore, seem to be a level at which everyone accepts that unemployment is a failure, and sees its reduction as a policy success. But it is unclear where the cut-off point is. As we have seen — in the cases of Denmark, Finland, France and West Germany — countries with governments who put greater emphasis on being more concerned with unemployment than the opposition does, may also embark on routes that lead to high unemployment.

Before we try to apply a yardstick of failure, we should look at the context of pressures and constraints, which the various governments have faced. Pressure will be defined in terms of labour-force growth, constraints in terms of the balance of payments situation, defined as the balance on current accounts. Both measures are admittedly crude, but they have two important advantages. Firstly, they are at once highly relevant to governmental policy, both in terms of popular demand and of governmental room to manoeuvre to meet those demands. Secondly, the availability of data makes it possible to compare these two indicators in a systemastic way.

The most clear-cut case where unemployment had a directly political cause is that of Britain. With low pressure and little immediate constraint — although, it should be admitted, with an ageing industrial structure and a long record of balance of payments problems — Britain has had the third largest rise in unemployment.

Table 36
Pressures and Constraints on High and Medium
Unemployment Countries[153]

Constraints	*Pressures*		
	High	*Medium*	*Low*
High	—	Australia	Belgium
		Denmark	France
		Finland	
		Italy	
Medium	Canada	—	Germany
Low	Netherlands	—	UK
	USA		

Constraints: medium=0.7-0.8 GDP percentage deficit for 1980-82, OECD average 0.5; lowest high constraint *de facto* 1.8 per cent (Finland); highest low constraint (USA), 0.0 per cent. High labour-force pressure ranging from 2 to 2.5 annual growth 1975-1983, medium 1.2-1.6, and low 0.3-0.5 per cent.

This is the record of the most consistently right-wing government under review. To judge from the murmurings and muted criticisms of the Confederation of British Industry and of certain Conservative politicians in late 1984 and 1985, that performance may also be considered a failure from a non-doctrinaire right-wing and business point of view. Among the left-of-centre regimes, the record of the West German Social Democrat–Liberal coalition is clearly the least successful, given low demographic pressure and the only medium balance of payments constraints. The Danish Social Democrat minority governments (until the right took power in late 1982) and the Finnish Social Democrat-led coalitions were facing the most difficult situation. The most left-wing government — that of France — confronted a situation of moderate difficulty. The failure of Francois Mitterrand is more blatant than that of Anker Jørgensen or of Mauno Koivisto and Kalevi Sorsa. Indeed, keeping in mind the relatively less developed character of the Finnish economy, the closing-off of the emigration solution, and the closeness to low unemployment rates, confirmed in developments in 1984, the Finns have not done too badly.

Economic context and political colour taken into account, Canada and Italy, although both clearly failing from a working-class point of view, come out rather better than might have been expected. Among the remaining countries, the Dutch failure is noteworthy — a massive increase of unemployment and a surplus of current accounts with the world. Here too, the bite of conservative government can be felt. The cases of Belgium — particularly bearing in mind the archaic industrial structure — and of the USA are less surprising, given the framework and the orientation of those governments. But in absolute terms, the performance of the Belgian state and of Belgian capitalism must be regarded as a clear failure, giving the country the highest rate of unemployment of any developed capitalist country.

It may legitimately be asked at this point, how do the low-unemployment countries fare in terms of pressures and constraints? The answer is as follows: Austria suffered average pressure with high constraint; Japan average pressure and low constraint; Norway high pressure and low constraint; Sweden low pressure and high constraint; Switzerland low pressure, low constraint. A crude additive index (from 2 to 6) gives an average for the low unemployment countries of 3.6 and for the rest of 4.2. But, looking at individual countries, Austria matches Australia, Denmark matches Finland, and Italy; Sweden matches France and Belgium; Norway faced a situation similar to that of the Netherlands and the USA; Japan had no real equivalent; Switzerland had, together with Britain, the easiest situation in the early 1980s. Clearly, factors other than demographic pressure and international economic constraint have to account for the differences between the low-unemployment countries and the rest.

Some failures are more interesting — politically as well as scientifically — than others. The failure of Thatcherism is most striking, but given its explicit priorities, hardly surprising. It is not, however, without its theoretical importance and bears eloquent witness to the fact that monetarism is incapable of paying its medium-term bills. This is also clear from the experience of Chile, where even the imposition of Friedmanite ideas onto the working class at gun-point — a measure not advocated by the Nobel Laureate himself — failed to produce the promised results. By contrast, the warfare-state Keynesianism of the Reagan Administration, with a federal budget deficit of about 20 per cent of expenditure in the fiscal year of 1984,[154] has been more successful. The most interesting or, if you want, intriguing, failures are elsewhere. They are of three sorts. One is the failure of left-wing or centre-left governments in Denmark, France and Germany. Another is that of the Netherlands, which although under right-wing rule, belongs — along with Austria and Switzerland — to the strongly consensual polities. Belgium has always had a character some way between the Netherlands and France, but here it is of particular interest, in being the country leading the way into the abyss of permanent mass unemployment. Thirdly, there is the case of Italy, where the failure has been surprisingly limited, given the weakness of the Italian economy before the crisis began, together with a far from consensual politics, and a Christian Democratic dominated political regime rather similar to those of Belgium and the Netherlands. Of these three, a special attention will be given to the Netherlands, because the generous Dutch welfare state actually provides something of a *Gestalt* to the notion — currently popular among certain sectors of the left or the ex-left—of 'liberation from work'.

The Danish Road to Unemployment.   Denmark is a progressive welfare state; this is expressed in high levels of social expenditure, of public employment, and of female participation in the labour force. Culturally and politically, it is also close to the two other countries of Scandinavia: Norway and Sweden. Indeed, before the Second World War, Denmark formed the social vanguard of the area. To find it today among the countries of mass unemployment is an intriguing phenomenon, enhanced by the fact that, for most of the crisis, Denmark has been governed by Social Democracy (although dependent on the centre parties for a majority). We already know that full employment never got the institutionalized standing it did in Norway and Sweden in the postwar period. The Danish state also always had a weaker grip on the economy than neighbouring states did, and there was no important public enterprise and little public control of the capital market.

The Danish economy entered the crisis in a weaker position than its neighbours. The historic Danish export sector was agricultural, and industrial enterprise was relatively small-scale, even after the wave of new industrialization in the sixties. The Danish economy has not acquired either the rather multifaceted transnational character of the Swedish engineering and timber-processing sectors, or the North Sea oil and gas wealth of the

Norwegians. The story of the crisis in Denmark cannot be told here, and there appears to be no other definitive study available. Instead, we will confine ourselves to outlining some problems and some of the inadequate policy responses.

Denmark has been plagued by constant balance of payments problems, which date from before the 1974-75 crisis. By 1982, the accumulated Danish deficit on current account, (30 per cent of GDP) was the highest among all advanced capitalist countries, surpassed in the OECD only by Ireland.[155] These problems, a rapidly growing public-sector deficit since the late seventies and the absence of any public grip over the volatile and highly speculative capital market, have led to a high interest-rate policy. Real interest rates have been far above the rest of the world, peaking at 10.6 per cent in 1978, going down to 5.2 per cent in 1980, then rising to 9.1 per cent in 1982 and 8.5 per cent in 1983.[156] In the 1979-82 period, this meant a real interest differential with the surrounding OECD countries of 4.7 per cent on average.[157] The pressure of growth in the labour force has been somewhat stronger than in OECD Europe — both in 1973-75 and in 1979-82 — but weaker than in the OECD as a whole.[158]

In the history of the crisis in Denmark there are two black years: 1974 and 1981. In the first year, (non-standardized) unemployment rose suddenly from 0.9 to 3.5 per cent, an unprecedented increase by international standards. In 1974 unemployment thus increased by 2.6 per cent, compared to 0.03 in the OECD as a whole and 1.2 in Germany. For the 1973-75 period as a whole, the Danes led the failures, with an unemployment growth of 4 per cent, compared with 1.9 for the OECD *in toto* and 3.6 for the USA — the next worst country.[159] In 1981, when Danish unemployment leaped from 7 to 9.2 per cent, Denmark was second to Thatcher's Britain, where joblessness rose from 6.9 to 10.6 per cent.[160]

The first plunge into the abyss was taken by the right-wing Liberal Hartling government in 1974. A restrictive fiscal policy increased unemployment. The direct effect of that was rather modest,[161] although the policy was remarkable as a way of confronting the mounting international crisis. More significant was the drastic reduction of the residential construction sector — part of a deliberate export sector re-orientation of the Danish economy.[162] Investment in residential construction declined by 24.7 per cent in 1974, a figure unique among developed capitalist countries.[163] Social Democratic minority governments have since pursued an expansive Keynesian fiscal policy, but one constantly counteracted by the tight monetary policy and high real interest rates. Thus, in 1976, the two policies almost cancelled each other — fiscal policy was calculated to have diminished unemployment by sixty thousand and high interest rates to have increased it by fifty-seven thousand. Since then, the balance has been more positive, but policies have still continued to work in opposite directions. In 1983, Danish econometricians estimate that fiscal policy reduced unemployment by one hundred and forty-six thousand (5.4 per cent of the labour force), while high interest rates increased it by forty-seven thousand (1.8 per cent of the labour force).[164] About a third of the 1981 rise in unemployment can be attributed to the interest rate situation — at 6.5 per cent the rate was 3.9 per cent higher than the average rate in neighbouring countries.[165] The rest of the increase may be due to the delayed effects of a structural decline of Danish industry, and since 1979, to drastically falling investment — particularly in agriculture, residential construction and in the public sector.[166] For some reason, the value of the Danish crown rose, and was allowed to rise, from 1972 to 1976, which — together with somewhat above the average wage increases — reduced Danish competitiveness. In 1976 this is estimated to have cost fifty-five thousand unemployed (2.2 per cent of the labour force). Only since 1981 have policies of international adjustment had a positive effect on unemployment.[167] Not too much should be made of these exercises in econometrics which are no doubt fascinating, for their practitioners. Norwegian currency revalued even more between 1972 and 1976, rising in value by 17 per cent (compared to 11 per cent for the Danish crown and a record 46 per cent for the Swiss franc).[168] The figures do, however, suffice to show that no consistent macro-economic policy was followed and further underline the far-reaching effects of government policy on employment levels.

In the first years of the crisis, the proportion of the workforce employed in the public sector in Denmark rose from 23 per cent in 1972 to 31 per cent in 1981.[169] There were, though, no public investment programmes as such, and labour-market policy was overwhelmingly geared to compensating for, rather than preventing, unemployment. About 8 per cent of labour market related expenditure went on cash benefits to the unemployed in 1979 — the figure for Sweden was a mere 10 per cent.[170] In 1981 only about 0.7 per cent of the workforce were employed on job creation schemes, this rose to 1.4 per cent in 1982.[171] Danish unemployment benefits are probably the most generous in the world, low wage earners get 90 per cent of their previous wage for two and a half years. Before the end of that period every claimant is offered a job (usually in the public sector) lasting for at least seven months, at the end of which the whole process can begin again. As in Sweden and Belgium, unemployment insurance is managed by funds linked to the unions, but unlike in Belgium these are mainly financed through public taxation.[172] It should, however, be noted that young people are often left without unemployment insurance cover — indeed 52 per cent of unemployed under twenty-five were not insured in 1979-82.[173] Even after the Job Offer Act (*Arbejdstilbudsloven*), the proportion of those employed through special employment programmes is less than half the Swedish figure.[174]

France: An Experience Repeated. If we put to one side the experience of fascism — which was certainly no side-show — there are a number of parallels between the post-1975 crisis and its predecessor of the thirties. These similarities are not only between broad developments — in Britain a divided Labour party gave way to stable Tory rule — but also in policy stances and directions. We can see this in the Netherlands where, both in the thirties and the eighties, a religious businessman presided over a hard currency policy and over a political line that emphasized the need to adjust to economic circumstances. Both in the Weimar Republic and in the postwar Federal Republic, balancing the budget and the national debt was a major concern. In Switzerland the consensus around giving priority to full employment for the native Swiss, has its parallels in the thirties. In the pre-Social Democratic Sweden of the thirties, the same scorn was shown for compensatory unemployment benefits as we saw in the post-Social Democratic Sweden of 1976-82.

Nowhere are the similarities more striking than in France. In 1936 the Popular Front government of Léon Blum committed itself to reducing unemployment through a reduction in working time and a boost in consumer demand, at the same time as maintaining the value of the franc (against the advice given by Hugh Dalton and Gunnar Myrdal).[175] The Popular Front ended in sharpened economic crisis, forced devaluation, internal division and demoralization. Apart from the working-class upsurge and the wave of factory occupations in the 1930s, the Mitterrand experience is fundamentally similar.

Mitterrand came to power largely on the basis of a campaign against unemployment.[176] There followed a wave of social security reforms, Keynesian reflation, nationalizations and employment-law reform. These measures were very far-reaching by French standards.[177] State-transfer payments to households increased by 5.8 per cent in 1981 and 7.8 per cent in 1982 in real terms. The real disposable income of households grew by 3.2 per cent in 1981 and 3.1 per cent in 1982.[178] It was also announced that the working week would be reduced to thirty-five hours with no loss of pay, although in the event only thirty-nine hours materialized in the autumn of 1981. It was not only through nationalization that the public sector expanded, but also through the extension of public services. Between 1975 and 1980, the yearly increase of employment in non-marketable services was 1.1 per cent, in 1981 it was 0.7 per cent, in 1982 1.7 per cent and in 1983 1.1 per cent again.[179] The French Socialists seem to have been banking on an upturn in the US economy in 1982 — in fact the cycle only peaked in 1984, with 1982 being a year of worldwide economic recession. The increase in domestic demand boosted foreign imports and mounting balance of payments pressure forced successive devaluations in October 1981, June 1982 and March 1983. Ever since then the government has put the brakes on demand and, as a result, real disposable household income fell by 0.3 per cent in 1983. Should we conclude that Mitterrand simply had bad luck, or must we draw the lesson that 'Keynesianism in One Country' is impossible, or that 'Keynes plus investment control' is *the* alternative, or that it also has proved to be a failure?[180]

In reality the issues are not so clear-cut. On the one hand, as the experience of the low-unemployment countries shows, the range of possible policies is greater than is usually imagined either on the left or on the right. On the other, we must seek to analyse the actual policies pursued in France in the context of the traditional national policy repertoire and the constraints actually faced.[181] Just as in 1936, the French Left of 1981 had three basic ideas about how to confront the crisis — all of them wrong. They were: short-term boosting of private consumption, a reduction in working time and the defence of the value of the currency. It could have been foreseen that there would be strong international pressure on a left-wing government in France. By 1980 there was already a current account deficit with the rest of the world,[182] and by 1979 inflation was 6.1 per cent higher than in West Germany, with the gap widening to 7.2 per cent in 1980.[183] The franc is linked to the Deutschmark through the European Monetary System. By the beginning of 1980, the discrepancy between the inflation rate of France and the (declining) average inflation rate of the fifteen main OECD countries was widening.[184]

Against this background, the decision to opt for an increase in consumption at the same time as defending the value of the franc was bound to fail. The series of devaluations came as last-minute reactions to pressure, rather than as moves to improve the competitiveness of the French economy.[185] Furthermore, the use of high interest rates to defend the currency — with real interest rates reaching around 7 per cent in the summer of 1981[186] acted as a disincentive to investment, which fell by 1.4 per cent in 1981.[187]

The lack of perseverance with expansionary policies on the part of the Mitterrand government is also remarkable. The strategy was at an end by March 1983. The reason for this about-turn was more political than economic. At least, we can judge this from the fact that France had more room to manoeuvre than several other advanced capitalist countries. In March 1983, Mitterrand announced that the budget deficit was not going to exceed 3 per cent of GDP.[188] Such a statement has to be evaluated in the light of the fact that the French deficit was 2.6 per cent in 1982, while the average for the seven big OECD economies was 4 per cent. At least by OECD standards, Mitterrand could not hold to his promise and in fact the deficit rose to 3.2 per cent in 1983 and 3.5 per cent in 1984. The average deficit for the 'Big Seven' was 4.1 per cent in 1983 and 3.4 per cent in 1984.[189] Government debt is much smaller in France than in the other major OECD countries — 32.4 per cent of GDP against a seven-countries average of 50.5 per cent.[190] In September 1983 Mitterrand announced that taxes and social security contributions would be reduced by one per cent of GDP, which, given the limit imposed on the budget deficit, meant cuts in public expenditure. This project received full expression in the 1985 Budget, which Minister of the Economy Beregovoy presents as 'neither reflationary nor deflationary' at a time when unemployment was above 9 per cent.[191] Between 1980 and 1983 taxes and compulsory social security contributions rose from 42.6

to 44.1 per cent of GDP, compared with an increase in Britain from 34.5 per cent in the 1978-79 fiscal year to 38.5 per cent in 1983-84. In other words, if Mitterrand achieves his goal he will have been much more effective at cutting taxes than Thatcher was in the first four years of her rule.[192]

Labour-market policy was not very developed in France before the crisis, and an EEC study of 1977 suggested that French policy and institutions were more backward in this respect than their German and British equivalents.[193] From 1977 a more active policy of counteracting unemployment was embarked upon, but the net effects seem to have been rather small.[194] Such policy as there was, was mainly compensatory in character. In 1980, expenditure on unemployment benefits alone constituted 54 per cent of what may be regarded as total French labour-market policy expenditure. Together with payment for advanced retirement, compensation expenditure amounted to 72 per cent.[195]

Labour-market pressure on the Mitterrand government has been relatively low. The labour force increased by 0.4 per cent in 1981 and by 0.8 per cent in the following year. Lowering of the normal retirement age and extensive early retirement plans *reduced* the French labour force by 0.5 per cent in 1983.[196] More active employment measures have been stepped up, but have remained far below Scandinavian levels. According to official French government figures, employment measures for maintaining special training programmes encompassed 0.7 per cent of the labour force in 1981, 1.1 per cent in 1982, and 1.2 per cent in 1983.[197]

In brief, the current high unemployment level in France can be explained neither in terms of the failure of left Keynesianism nor in terms of the impossibility of fighting the crisis in one country alone. The Mitterrand government has failed to keep unemployment down, mainly because of its own contradictory policies. To explain the particular form of those internal policy contradictions and of the sharp shifts of line would require a special analysis of recent French socio-political history. That task is outside the framework of this study. But this much is clear: the main reason for the miserable French employment record from 1981 to 1984 is to be sought in historically institutionalized patterns of politics, not in economic theory or international dependence.

Germany: A Strong Economy's and a Strong Social Democracy's Road to Unemployment. West Germany ceased to be a country of full employment in 1975, when unemployment rose from 1.6 to 3.6 per cent. By the criteria of the 1980s, that is not very high, but it turned out to be a watershed, which meant that Germany has — at least for fifteen years and perhaps forever — parted company with Austria, Japan, Norway, Sweden and Switzerland. This was an unexpected development, given the strength of the German economy and the country's Social Democrat dominated government.

It is true, however, that indications of a slowdown in the economy had become visible just before the crisis. German growth figures in 1971-73 were lower than the OECD, EEC and 'Big Seven' averages. In 1974 German economic growth was faster than the Big Seven as a whole, but worse than the OECD and the EEC. In 1975 the economy of the Federal Republic performed below all the averages just mentioned, but bettered all of them in 1976. Unemployment, however, continued to rise. During the period of 1974-82, the German economy grew by 1.7 per cent each year compared to 1.9 per cent for the EEC, 1.6 per cent for the 'Big Seven' and 1.4 per cent for Sweden.[198] On the international front the Germans remained strong. In 1974 West Germany was, after the Netherlands, the only OECD country which had a substantial surplus on current transactions with the rest of the world and, together with only the USA, Netherlands and Switzerland, ran a surplus for both 1974 and 1975.[199]

If the international constraints were not severe, the same is true of pressure resulting from the growth in the labour force. In 1973 the German workforce increased by 0.3 per cent, compared with an EEC average of 0.9 per cent and an OECD figure of 1.8 per cent. In 1974, the German labour supply *decreased* by 0.7 per cent, unmatched even in Switzerland, while the EEC and the OECD work forces increased by 0.3 and 1.3 per cent. In 1975, largely thanks to an offensive against the *gastarbeiter,* the German labour force declined by a further 1.5 per cent, less than in Switzerland (−5.0 per cent), but unrivalled elsewhere.[200]

Nor were political resources and policies lacking. Germany was governed by a Social Democratic-dominated coalition, committed to social reform, Keynesian economic management, and full employment. The Grand Coalition of 1966-69 between Christian and Social Democracy had left two important political resources: a belatedly adopted but generally successful experience of Keynesian crisis management and an institutionalization of labour-market policy (through the Work Promotion Act of 1969) which at the time had no rival outside Sweden. Federal and other public-sector policies worked together, thereby increasing total government deficit spending from 1.3 per cent of GDP in 1974 to 5.7 per cent in 1975.[201]

Active labour-market policies, involving special training and work programmes and, above all, subsidized short-time and bad weather work, were unleashed. Such measures covered 2.5 per cent of the labour force in 1975 — a figure even higher than in Sweden.[202]

Why then did high unemployment occur? Immediate responsibility can be quite clearly placed at the feet of the Federal Bank (*Bundesbank*) which both by statute and custom has a much greater autonomy from the government than the national banks of the full employment countries (with the possible exception of Switzerland). The Federal Bank was in charge of the whole range of monetary policy which, after the free floating of exchange rates in March 1983, was considerably widened in scope. The bank used this to implement a full-fledged restrictive policy, running directly counter to government fiscal and labour-market policies from 1974 on.[203] The concrete expression of German Federal Bank policy was that real interest rates (short-term as well as long-term) were higher in Germany in 1974 and 1975 than in any other advanced capitalist country.[204] The result of this policy is most immediately visible in investment (gross fixed capital formation), which declined by 3.5 per cent of GDP between 1973 and 1975, compared to a figure of 1.9 per cent among the 'Big Seven' countries, 1.5 per cent in the EEC, and 1.8 per cent in the OECD.[205]

This restrictive stance of the German Federal Bank can only be fully evaluated against the background of three sets of facts. First, the mark was strong, and there was a surplus in the transactions with the rest of the world (a very rare phenomenon in non-OPEC countries at the time). Secondly, by the international standards of the time, German inflation was very low (lower in 1973 than all OECD countries except Luxemburg, the USA and Sweden). In 1974 and 1975 Germany had the lowest inflation of any of the twenty-four OECD countries.[206] Thirdly, high real interest rates are a discouragement to investment, and the West German rate of investment fell from a high level in 1971 to a point below the 'Big

Seven', EEC and OECD averages in 1974.[207]

We are not able to probe into the minds of the governors of the German Federal Bank. Nevertheless we may conclude that their policy was a free choice, not dictated by any economic necessity, and was the most important determinant of the rise of unemployment in West Germany. What the Social Democratic–Liberal Coalition could have done about the Federal Bank if it had tried, is unclear. What is known, however, is that no consistent policy of full employment was pursued by that government.

The absence of an institutionalization of a commitment to full employment led to stop-go policies, which 'created uncertainty, led firms to believe that measures were only temporary and not worth adjusting to'.[208] The 1981-82 downturn was met by the government with a *deflationary* fiscal policy. Government budgets decreased deficit spending by 0.2 per cent of GDP in 1981 and by 1.5 per cent in 1982, the latter being the product of an explicit austerity programme — 'Operation 82' — launched in January 1982.[209] The background to this was partly that West Germany had run into a deficit in her current transactions with the rest of the world in 1979-81. It was not a serious deficit by international standards, but was aggravated by adverse long-term capital movements (outward investment) in 1982, when the current account returned to surplus.[210] Cuts and more stringent rules were adopted in 1981-82 with regard to policies towards the unemployed.[211] German labour-market policy had all the time been mainly compensatory — cash unemployment benefits comprising 80 per cent of labour-market policy expenditure in 1975.[212]

Available time-series data further show that the depression of 1982 (with an unemployment rate of 6.1 per cent), was countered by a labour-market policy no more extensive than in 1975.[213] If the subsidization of short-time work is included, governmental labour-market intervention in 1982 was somewhat less than in 1975. If only job creation (*Arbeitsbeschaffung*) and vocational retraining programmes are considered, German active labour-market policy was scaled down in 1982, compared to 1981, from employing one hundred and seventy-four thousand to one hundred and sixty-six thousand people.[214] The disgraceful end of the Schmidt government is underlined by the fact that the number of people employed on job creation programmes under Helmut Kohl in 1984 was slightly higher than in 1982 (seventy thousand against sixty-seven thousand).[215]

The West German road to stable high unemployment was first opened by the restrictive policies of the Federal Bank in 1974-75, against which the erratic government policies of the Social Democratic-Liberal coalition proved ineffective. The trend was deepened by the deflationary fiscal and decelerated labour-market policies of the coalition in 1982. Little wonder that the German Social Democrats went down to defeat. For a left-of-centre government to pursue right-wing policies does not pay.

Italian Intermezzo. Unemployment in Italy rose less between 1974 and 1983 than in any other high unemployment country, except the USA and Finland. Furthermore, Italy and the USA were the only high unemployment countries in which unemployment rose less than was to be expected by changes in the supply of labour and economic growth. We have already noted that under the premiership of the Social Democrat Craxi, Italy in 1984 joined the group of countries whose unemployment is above 10 per cent. Even so, up to the mid-1980s, the Italian economy has shown remarkable vigour, and joblessness remains well below Belgian, Dutch, British and Canadian rates.

This outcome was hardly to be expected. Italy has long been a high unemployment country, with 6.3 per cent unemployment in 1972. In 1973 Italy ran a deficit on current account with the rest of the world of 1.8 per cent of GDP.[216] The state had acquired a net public-sector borrowing requirement of 5 per cent of GDP in 1970, rising to 8.1 per cent in 1974 — a figure unmatched elsewhere in the capitalist world.[217] The increase of unit labour costs (in manufacturing) was higher in Italy for the 1972-82 period than in any other country under review.[218] So why has Italy done much better in the crisis, than, say, Britain or the Netherlands?

To be frank, no more than a hypothesis can be offered here as an explanation. Like Austria (and Finland to some extent), Italy in the 1970s was catching up with and joining the most developed capitalist countries. In Italy, this process of modernization was significantly spurred on by the social upheavals and the dramatic growth of the labour movement around 1970. Thus, productivity rose strongly, profits remained high in spite of rising labour costs, manufacturing employment remained largely stable, and the previously low service employment increased above the Western

European average.[219]

The large publicly-owned business sector maintained employment levels relative to its private competitors more vigorously than was the case in Austria.[220] The lira was devalued by 15 per cent against the dollar in 1973, thereby establishing a competitive international position until 1980.[221] Real interest rates were allowed to become negative in the second half of the 1970s.[222] Total government outlays increased by 15.9 per cent between 1973 and 1982 — to be compared with an EEC average of 11.1 per cent and an OECD figure of 9.2 per cent.[223]

Capitalist modernization and innovation, with a large increase of new businesses[224] (many of them sweatshops), and expansive public policy without any significant labour-market policy, seem to have combined in producing the less than disastrous Italian record. In the mid-1980s, tight monetary and restrictive fiscal policies are predictably leading to increased unemployment.[225]

Italian unemployment has a particular structure. It is mainly youth unemployment, reflecting an archaic educational system, poorly attuned to the labour market, and the absence of any substantial active labour-market policy. In 1984, about one third of all Italian youth (14-24) were unemployed, an unequalled failure among developed Western countries. By contrast, adult unemployment — prevented by strong trade unions and trade union-induced protective policies — is lower at about 4.5 per cent in 1984 than in any other country, except the five nations with low unemployment.[226] No wonder that class analysis and class politics are being seriously questioned on the Italian left. But whether any legitimate theoretical and strategic conclusions may be extrapolated from one peculiar experience is another matter. With regard to unemployment, the importance of the state and its policies is once again reaffirmed — quite contrary to the Italian infatuation with theories of 'ungovernability' as well as the compatibility of such a role with vigorous private capitalism.

The Ways of Doom

Three countries are outstanding in their failure — Britain, Belgium and the Netherlands. The record of the British Labour Party on unemployment is rather tarnished, but Britain's location at the bottom of the league is a post-1979 phenomenon. In that year unemployment rose sharply from 5.6 per cent to 6.9 per cent in 1980, 10.6 per cent in 1981 and 13.5 per cent in 1984.[227] Over the same time-span, pressure from the labour supply completely ceased. International constraints also eased in the 1980s with Britain running a significant surplus on current account in 1980-83.[228] The failure of the most doctrinaire right-wing government among democratic capitalist countries on the unemployment front could hardly have been more spectacular. However, it is so obvious that a society and an economy of full employment and participation is not the goal of Thatcher and her acolytes that an enumeration of those of her policies that have been destructive of jobs would simply be banal. 'Thatcherism' is first and foremost a problem of political strategy.[229]

Belgian Gloom. The increase of unemployment in Belgium during the crisis has been the highest of any of our sixteen countries. It was also, after Swiss full employment, the development least accounted for by a combination of economic growth and labour-supply increase. Three sets of factors appear to account for the Belgian employment disaster. The first, probably least important given the fact that in 1980 only 26 per cent of the employed Belgian labour force worked in industry (exclusive of construction),[230] is economic structure. In part one we found that Belgium in 1975 had a disproportionate amount of her manufacturing employment located in crisis-affected branches: steel and textiles. More significant, however, are the effects of a uniquely high level of international dependence. The sum of merchandise exports and imports exceeded Gross Domestic Product by 33 per cent in 1982. International dependence has combined with industrial structure to hit Belgian employment; this has been further exacerbated by the third factor — pay and currency policy.

In spite of the deep and deepening crisis of traditional Belgian industry, in spite of the high unemployment (above the EEC average since 1975), and in spite of Belgian dependence on foreign trade, the Belgian National Bank opted for a hard currency policy. Against recurring pressure, the Belgian franc was continuously revalued throughout the 1970s, with small, forced depreciations in 1980 and 1981. The inevitable devaluation came in 1982.[231] That this policy was maintained, even though Belgium had been losing her share of overseas markets since 1974 and was, since 1977, running an increasing deficit on her current account with the rest of the world — a deficit far above OECD and EEC averages — should tell us something about the strength of Belgian banking capital.[232]

Belgium is similar to Britain, not only in following the UK as the second most industrialized country in the world, but also in the sense of having her industrial capital clearly subordinate to — but not separate from — banking and finance. Inflation in Belgium was below the OECD average throughout the 1970s, apart from 1972 and 1975-76.[233] But collective bargaining was quite successful for employed Belgian workers and employees. Between 1978 and 1982, Belgium was alone among the seven small countries of Scandinavia, the Low Countries, Austria and Switzerland, in having a real wage increase — one per cent per annum. But the picture has now changed, in 1982 real wages declined by 3.9 per cent.[234] By 1981, real wage increases were exceeding rises in productivity — adjusted for changes in terms of trade — by 16 per cent (calculated on the basis of 1972 figures), compared to 8 per cent in Switzerland and France, and −2 per cent in Germany.[235] The result was an extreme import elasticity. A one per cent change in national income in the period of 1977-82 meant a 1.37 per cent increase in imports, compared to 1.21 per cent in Japan, 1.2 per cent in Germany, 1.14 per cent in the Netherlands and in Sweden, 0.99 per cent in the USA and 0.84 per cent in the UK.[236] Domestic demand has declined, and in 1981-82 residential construction fell by 45 per cent.[237]

Policies have had their negative impact on unemployment even apart from their effect on the competitive position of an extremely dependent country. The frantic efforts to bolster up the currency — and the public-sector deficit — led to high real interest rates, with corresponding effects on investment. At 4.2 per cent in 1978, 5.2 per cent in 1979 and 7.6 per cent in 1980, Belgian real interest rates were second only to Danish ones.[238] While monetary policy actively generated unemployment, fiscal policy was passive and neutral. Before the crisis Belgium had already developed a public-sector deficit, that had become structural (instead of counter-cyclical) and which grew further in the wake of increasing unemployment. Calculated on a full-employment basis, the public-sector deficit remained constant, at 2 per cent of GDP, throughout 1974-78.[239]

Full employment was never institutionalized in Belgium, and such labour-market policy that there was, was *exclusively* compensatory in character. But with the entry of the Social Democrats into the government in May 1977, a change took place. Compensatory labour-market expenditure had decreased to a mere 57 per cent of all such expenditure by 1980.[240] At their peak in late 1979, active labour-market measures employed 2.6 per cent of the labour force.[241]

However, since January 1982, Belgium has been governed by a right-wing Christian Democratic–Liberal coalition, the main orientation of which is austerity and the reduction of the public-sector deficit.[242] While unemployment is rising and real wages are declining real income from property and entrepreneurship is growing and share yields are soaring;[243] between August 1982 and August 1983 these were at 11 per cent in Belgium. Comparable figures are France with 5.4 per cent, Netherlands 5.0 per cent, UK 4.8 per cent, USA 4.4 per cent, Germany 4.3 per cent. Swedish shares gave, on average, 2 per cent and Japanese ones 1.4 per cent.[244] At the same time unemployment benefits have been reduced.[245] Generous entitlements to, but not particularly high amounts of, unemployment benefits[246] compensate, in part, for the disastrous outcome of a weak and internationally dependent economy, a weak and divided state, the power of finance capital, and restrictive government policies. While some people are reaping ample profits, most Belgians seem to be doomed to a situation of further deterioration, unless the policies of the current right-wing Christian Democrat–Liberal government are drastically changed.

Netherlands: What Happens While Waiting for a Miracle. The Netherlands ceased to be a country enjoying full employment from the first onset of the international crisis. Internationally standardized unemployment rates stayed in the range of 5.2-5.5 per cent throughout the second half of the 1970s.[247] This was hardly to be expected from the economic and political situation of the Netherlands in the mid-1970s. For the 1974-76 period, Dutch economic growth (2.6 per cent per annum), clearly surpassed OECD (1.7 per cent) and EEC (1.8 per cent) averages.[248] In 1977-79 the Dutch economy grew somewhat more slowly than the international average, but still at a respectable rate — 2.4 per cent. In all of the first years of the crisis (1974-76), the Dutch had a surplus in their transactions with the rest of the world, unrivalled by any other OECD country and, except for a small deficit in 1978-80, they have been running a surplus ever since.[249] Labour-force pressure was at first relatively low, an annual increase of 0.4 per cent in 1973-76, as compared with 0.5 per cent in the EEC and 1.3 per cent in the OECD.[250] In the latter half of the 1970s the Dutch labour force, very small in relation to the adult population, increased significantly in numbers.[251]

Politically, the Netherlands was at the same time experiencing her most progressive developments since 1918. At last, the hard crust of institutionalized religion was cracking. Tight social control was breaking up, and the Netherlands became what she now is, an unusually permissive society. Secularization swept through welfare institutions, trade unions and political parties. The Catholic hierarchy was the main loser, with the Catholic Party losing heavily in the elections. The Catholic trade union merged with the Social Democratic one. Both the Catholic and the Calvinist churches themselves took a daring turn towards broad-minded social and political concern. In office was the most progressive parliamentary government the Dutch have ever had. It was a cabinet led by the Social Democrats, in coalition with the Catholics and the Calvinist Anti-Revolutionaries — who in spite of their name, denoting their resistance to the French revolution in 1789 (!), had become fairly progressive — and two new left-of-centre parties (D'66 and PPR).

What went wrong? A brief answer is that a hesitant and ambiguous government response to the crisis and the underlying structural weaknesses of the Dutch economy combined to lay the foundations for one of the most spectacular employment failures in the developed capitalist world. The Dutch economy had always employed only a relatively small part of the population — in 1970 the figure was 57.3 per cent of the population aged fifteen to sixty-four, lower than any country except Greece and Italy (the EEC average was then 64.9 per cent).[252] In spite of this, Dutch employment had decreased by 0.9 per cent in 1972, after which it stagnated in 1973 and 1974. This pre-crisis pattern was unique in the OECD world, although Italy had a larger decline of employment in 1972 that was more than compensated for in 1973 and 1974.[253] A sharp decline in industrial employment was not fully counteracted by a growth in service-sector employment.[254] Another indicator of pre-crisis labour-market malaise was the growth of the number of disabled (*arbeidsongeschikten*). Between 1963 and 1973, the number of beneficiaries of disability pensions (*WAO-uitlkeringen*) almost doubled, from one hundred and eighty-three thousand to three hundred and fifty-three thousand; from somewhat above 4 per cent of the labour force to somewhat above 7 per cent.[255] Behind this official growth of disability there must have been hidden unemployment.

The expansionist policy response to the crisis was modest. Dutch deficit spending in 1975 increased by 2.6 per cent of GDP, as against 3.8 per cent in Austria and 4.4 per cent in Germany. Labour-market policy was also modest. Anti-cyclical public works and training programmes covered 0.3 per cent of the Dutch labour force at the height of such policy in 1976 (a somewhat lower figure than the USA's 0.4 per cent).[256]

With regard to providing work for the handicapped (which is included in the Swedish total for active labour-market measures), the Dutch record is much better. In 1980 jobs provided for the handicapped amounted to 1.6 per cent of the labour force.[257] The Swedes, in comparison, provided 'protected work' for 1.2 per cent of their labour force in 1980, a figure which corresponds to 1.8 per cent of a labour force the size of the Dutch one.[258] At their peak, in 1976, Dutch labour-market employment and training measures cost 0.46 per cent of GDP, while Sweden spent 1.8 per cent of GDP in 1975/76 and 3.1 per cent in 1977-78.[259]

Behind this mediocre policy response to the crisis were an independent central bank headed by a Calvinist former prime minister and a divided government. The division was not, as in Germany, between fiscal and labour-market policy, on the one hand, and monetary policy on the other. Dutch real interest rates were allowed to become negative in this first period of the crisis.[260] The division was within the Cabinet itself. A special, very negative role, was also played by the supreme economic body of the Dutch state, the Central Planbureau. Divisions in the Cabinet seem to have run not along party but along portfolio lines. The main spokesman for an expansionist, employment-oriented policy was the Calvinist Anti-Revolutionary Minister for Social Affairs and Employment Boersma. His most important opponent was Social Democratic Minister of Finance Duisenberg — today President of the Netherlands National Bank — who was against the modest 'stimulation packages' which were adopted. Duisenberg prevailed, and in the autumn of 1975, a 'one per cent operation' was adopted upon his suggestion. According to this proposal the growth of taxation and social insurance premiums should be limited to no more than 1 per cent of GDP each year. Employment, at least in the short term, was a secondary concern.[261]

At the same time, the hesitant policies of the government with regard to unemployment got an unanimous thumbs-down in January 1975 from the advisory Council of the Labour Market, a body composed of employers, trade-union representatives and government-appointed experts.[262] Indeed, in 1976, current receipts of the Dutch government (including gas taxes) increased only 0.4 per cent of GDP, then declined by 1.5 per cent in 1977.[263]

In spite of the manoeuvres of Duisenberg, full employment remained a major goal of the Den Uyl government. This was expressed in the policy document on employment presented to parliament in early 1975.[264] Added to the government policy document was an appendix from the Central Planbureau on the development of structural unemployment. It argued that unemployment was due to rising labour costs.[265] The theoretical backbone of this stance, which later contributed to the econometric computer model of the Planbureau, was a paper by H. den Hartog and H.S. Tjan,[266] which is probably the single most important scientific contribution to the understanding of current mass unemployment in the Netherlands.

The basic idea of den Hartog and Tjan, developing a model by Robert Solow, was that the demand for labour is determined by the age, the 'vintage' of what Marx would call 'constant capital' — or in den Hartog and Tjan's terminology 'outillage' — and that the lifetime of this capital is determined by real labour costs. In brief, the higher the labour costs, the more rapidly constant capital is replaced and rejuvenated and, given technological progress, the less labour per unit of constant capital/outillage will be demanded. Being no econometrician, I see no point in going into further details of the model nor of waging a battle on the terrain of econometrics. More relevant are the conclusions we can draw from it about the problem of unemployment.

As an explanation, the contribution of den Hartog and Tjan is no more than a *post hoc, ad hoc* interpretation of the 1959-73 period. The model cannot cope with sectoral shifts in the economy, for instance between manufacturing and services, the latter requiring little constant capital. Because of this, the authors honestly admit that they had to abandon their original plan of applying their model to the whole postwar period. Important sectoral shifts before 1959 made the model irrelevant. No role is allocated to the state and to any kind of public policy, which to some of us at least, is a rather surprising assumption of economists working for a public Planbureau. In the elaborate econometric model used by the Planbureau, 'Vintaf II', special public employment projects by the state were also put into the computer, with the assumption that they would in the medium or long run *increase* employment, because of the adverse effects of taxation. This thesis, technically expressed in saying that the 'balanced budget multiplier' was negative, derived from a matching of the econometric equation to data for the 1951-74 developments in the Netherlands. However, if 1953 had been taken as the basis year the multiplier would have come out positive, showing that public employment projects can indeed have a positive effect against unemployment.[267] A model which has been made to fit one particular case can, of course, make no scientifically legitimate claim to being anything more than a hypothesis about the determinants of employment. In fact, in a simple comparative test the model fails.

While comparative data are available for exactly the same period, if we take the five years preceding the crisis of 1974 a certain picture appears. Manufacturing employment — which should be the most favourable ground to test the model — *declined* in the Netherlands by 0.9 per cent annually while unit labour costs rose 0.6 per cent. At the same time, in the EEC as a whole manufacturing employment *rose* by 0.6 per cent per annum and unit labour costs by 0.7 per cent .[268] The Planbureau argument that *x* per cent wage increase means *y* per cent unemployment assumes, without saying, that given institutions and expectations are unchangeable.[269]

The reason for such types of argument is not to be sought in any particular school of economic science but in the political and economic history of the Netherlands. Postwar economic policy was geared to the industrialization and economic development of an economy that was, by Western European standards, not very developed. A 'directed (low) wage policy' (*geleidde loonpolitiek*), was administered by the state in a corporatist manner, as the major instrument of planning.[270] By 1964 the Dutch workers had had enough and a 'wage explosion' ensued. For most Dutch economists and for a large number of politicians, the controlled low-wage era still represents a Golden Age. 1964 was explicitly picked out as a crucial year in the cool econometric studies of den Hartog and Tjan. To this day Dutch economists tend to regard the end of the state-controlled low-wage economy as the 'Fall from Grace' and the beginning of the current crisis of the Netherlands.[271]

The effect of the labour cost argument upon the development of unemployment in the Netherlands has been disastrous for two reasons. First, since there is in fact no direct and unambiguous relationship between labour cost and unemployment developments, as our analysis has shown. It has meant a concentration on a wrong or, put more cautiously, rather sterile path. Secondly, it has served as a theoretical and ideological justification for the state playing an increasingly passive role in the face of the mounting problems of mass unemployment. Indeed, the criteria for evaluating joblessness have been lowered to an amazing extent. In a retirement interview, the director of the Central Planbureau for many years, C.A. van der Beld, called the 1984 employment trend 'brilliant' (*schitterend*), referring to the fact that in 1983 nine hundred thousand unemployed were predicted for 1984 (over 15 per cent of the labour force), while in September 1984 there were only eight hundred and thirty thousand (just over 14 per cent) and no higher figure was expected in 1985![272]

After the failure of the hesitant and divided Den Uyl Cabinet (1973-77) and a couple of uneventful and under-used years, the Dutch economy has taken a disastrous course in the 1980s. Economic growth in 1980-84, at about 0.7 per cent a year, was the lowest of all the sixteen countries.[273] At the same time, the labour force increased much more than in any other country, partly because of the maturing effects of previously high fertility rates and partly because of increased female participation in the labour market.[274] Mass unemployment surged over the country, leaping from six per cent in 1980 to 8.6 per cent in 1981, 11.4 per cent in 1982, and 13.7 per cent in 1983, resting at about fourteen per cent in 1984, and likely to stay around that level in 1985.[275]

We found in part one that economic growth and labour-force development could explain only twelve per cent of the wide national variations of unemployment after 1974. But for individual countries, the fit is better. Two thirds of the 1974-83 Dutch unemployment increase could be accounted for by labour force and overall economic growth combined. Other things being equal, if the Dutch labour force had only grown at the same rate as the Swedish one between 1979-1983, Dutch unemployment would have been 7.6 per cent in 1983 instead of 13.7 per cent — an increase of 2.2 per cent instead of 8.3 per cent.[276]

On the other hand, Dutch unemployment figures are lowered by the high proportion of the population aged 15-64 who do not take part in the labour market at all (at least the registered labour market). If Dutch labour-force participation in 1981 had been the same as in Sweden but all else remained equal, Dutch unemployment would have been 39 per cent, instead of 8.6 per cent.[277]

The Dutch economy has operated under no severe international constraints. There has been surplus on transactions with the rest of the world for most of the time, and even when a small deficit (1.1 and 1.5 per cent of GDP) developed in 1980 and 1981, this was below the OECD average (−2.5 and −1.9 per cent).[278]

In the face of these developments, Dutch government policy has had two main ingredients. Firstly to *restrict* demand and employment by reducing public expenditure and public-sector employment; secondly, to do nothing, while waiting for a miracle, called 'a new industrial elan'. The intellectual architect of this foolproof recipe for rising and permanent unemployment is the (recently retired) chairman of Royal Dutch Shell, G. Wagner. Wagner was the chairman and central figure of two public advisory commissions on industrial and economic policy, putting out a series of extremely influential reports in 1980-83.[279] Apart from the then chairman of Shell, the commission included a senior manager of Unilever, the head of the Netherlands' largest retail concern, a senior manager of Philips and a manager from the Netherlands' largest bank, together with token trade unionists. As special experts the director of the Planbureau and the latter's vice-director were also included.

Political responsibility for all this falls to the right-wing Christian Democrats and the right-wing Liberals, who have been governing the Netherlands since 1978, except for a crisis-ridden Christian Democratic–Social Democratic coalition in 1981-82.

The main task of the state has been seen as increasing profitability in private enterprise. Profitability is largely seen as spatially determined. The public sector has to be cut back, in order to provide more 'space' for private business. Even in its documents on employment, the Dutch government asserts as its primary task a retraining of the public sector.[280] The logic is basically the same as that of the Social Democratic Finance Minister Duisenberg in the mid-1970s, only now it has whole-hearted Cabinet backing.

Between 1975-76 and 1980-82 Dutch public expenditure increased from 53.4 per cent of GDP to 61.6 per cent, mainly as a result of transfer payments. Over the same period public consumption increased by 0.5 per cent and public investment *fell* by 0.9 per cent. Public revenue only increased from 51.5 per cent to 56.1 per cent — an increase of 4.6 per cent of which 2.9 per cent was contributed by gas revenue and 1.9 by social security contributions. Business taxation has decreased from 3.2 to 3.1 per cent and income-related household taxes from 11.7 per cent to 11.0 per cent.[281] The deficit, lower in 1983 than that of Belgium, Italy and Denmark, is thus a result of a contradictory government policy,[282] on one hand keeping taxes down for business and high income earners, on the other maintaining an expensive welfare state, which pays generously for job losses. Given the ban on increased taxation, government policy has been concentrated on reducing the deficit by cuts. No 'deficit-increasing' employment policies have been deemed acceptable.[283] Therefore, in a country of mass unemployment, the government congratulates itself on having brought public employment to a standstill,[284] and has even agreed to cut it further in 1983-86.[285]

That this policy would cause mass unemployment was clear to those responsible for it and was made quite explicit in the budget debate in the Dutch parliament. In the autumn of 1980 Premier Van Agt (a right-wing Catholic Christian Democrat) made it clear that he saw no solution to unemployment 'at least in the coming decade ... and perhaps not even after that.' Van Agt took Social Democratic leader Den Uyl to task for irresponsibly demanding full employment or, as Van Agt preferred to put it, 'that you can only completely, humanely and socially function in society (*meefunctionerend*), when you have acquired a paid job.'[286]

The short-lived centre-left coalition of 1981-82 did add an appendix about an employment programme (*bijstelling*) to the prepared budget for 1982.[287] Complacency was not a Christian Democratic monopoly. In the budget debate in the autumn of 1981, the main Social Democratic spokesman on economic affairs Wölfgens, congratulated his compatriots by saying: 'The new policy provides an unique experiment in macro-economic policy, compared with the rest of the industrialized world; an exercise in equilibrium (*evenwichtsbalkoefening*) between a withdrawal of collective claims (*beslag*) and a directed attack (*aanpak*) on unemployment'.[288] A governmental answer to a question in parliament in 1982 about the consequences for employment of the economic strategy stated that 'in no other OECD country hitherto has such a plan been developed as the Dutch one, which starts from a systematic co-ordination of all the forms of policy which have an influence upon the development of employment.'[289] To appreciate this statement in full, the reader should know two things. Firstly, the effect of government policy on employment for 1981 that was reported in the answer corresponded to 0.2 per cent of the labour force, this being about 58 per cent of what was achieved by the Carter administration in USA, and 5.5 per cent of the best Swedish effort. Secondly, the figure does not take into account the mobility promoting measures and the jobs for the handicapped provided by the Dutch government, nor local government initiatives.

In spite of massive unemployment, there is little blatant poverty in the Netherlands. Dire poverty, if it exists, is largely invisible, even in a city like Nijmegen with an unemployment rate above 25 per cent. The main reason — no doubt supplemented by a 'black economy' — is the generosity of the Dutch welfare state. In 1983, 36 per cent of disposable household income in the Netherlands was composed of public transfers, in 1979 it was 30.5 per cent.[290] In Sweden in 1979 transfer benefits amounted to 33 per cent of disposable household income, but it should be noted that the proportion of old people is much higher in Sweden. If Sweden had the same proportion of old people as the Netherlands among its population — 71 per cent of its actual proportion in 1980 — other things being equal, the share of transfer benefit in household disposable income in Sweden would have been 27.7 per cent. In Britain transfer payments amounted to 24.7 per cent of household disposable income in 1979, and 27.6 per cent in 1981, of which roughly thirty per cent was made up by private pensions and annuities. With the same proportion of old people as Holland (aged sixty-five and over), the percentages would have been 23.0 and 25.6 respectively.[291] Unemployment and assistance benefits are high by international standards, although cuts will be made in 1985, as some were in 1984. In the second half of 1983, the total effect of transfer payments averaged out among different kinds of benefits for different duration and type of unemployment was a twenty per cent loss of income for the average (modal) worker/ employee and an income equivalent to the minimum wage for an unemployed person with a non-working partner. A single person, on average wages, lost 43 per cent of his/her income. For an eighteen-year-old who could argue that he or she was living alone, it actually paid to be unemployed in comparison with taking a minimum wage job (a benefit of one per cent), but if someone with a working partner became unemployed then they would lose everything in relation to both the minimum and the average wage.[292]

Social assistance for a couple is equal to the minimum wage (for adults), for single-parent families it is nine-tenths and for single persons seven-tenths of the minimum wage (in 1984).[293] For a couple the Dutch assistance level in early 1985 is 1471 guilders a month, which is about the same as £358 or 3100 Swedish crowns a month (figures are exclusive of child allowances, rent subsidies and lump sum benefits).[294]

By comparison, in Sweden assistance levels vary by as much as a factor of two from one municipality to another.[295] The advisory norm of the National Social Board, put out in December 1984 gives about 2900 crowns for a couple (about 1145 guilders a month), although domestic purchasing power may not quite correspond to bank exchange rates.[296] Pensions, on the other hand, are higher in Sweden than in the Netherlands. In early 1985, a Swedish pensioned couple, having no rights under the 1958 general superannuation scheme, would have a basic pension of 4596 crowns a month, about 1815 guilders, or £442 a month. Dutch old age pensioners would receive, for a married couple, 1546 guilders plus 93 guilders vacation benefit a month in early in 1985. Because of the lack of any general scheme of supplementary occupational pensions in the Netherlands, there is no possibility of making a direct comparison between the most commonly encountered actual pension levels in the two countries. For those particularly interested, we may observe however that a single old age pensioner in Sweden with a normal occupational pension got (on top of the basic pension) about 1617 guilders or £394 a month (4096 crowns) in early 1985.[297]

Dutch state policy has two basic socio-economic features. On one hand, a passive economic policy, mainly aimed at diminishing the role of the state still further in order to provide 'space' (*ruimte*) for the private sector. On the other, a generous social policy, trying to compensate for the failures of Dutch capitalism and Dutch economic policy by paying social benefits to the mounting number of unemployed and 'disabled' (most of whom are really just unemployed). In the first quarter of 1984 seven hundred and thirty-four thousand Dutchmen were receiving disability benefits — a number that corresponds to 12.6 per cent of the labour force.[298] Of the income receivers in the Netherlands in 1983 who were *below the normal pension age*, 51 per cent derived their income from the market sector, 22 per cent from state and para-state employment, and 27 per cent were living on social security and social assistance benefits.[299] One aspect of this double policy is an institution which in Dutch is called '*werk met behoud van uitkering*'. Literally translated it means 'work with maintenance of social benefits'. It refers to the possibility for unemployed people who receive welfare payments to work gratis, mainly in local social services. It is calculated that about a hundred thousand people are doing unpaid work for the state and para-state institutions (about 1.7 per cent of the labour force). It seems that only someone who is not Dutch can see anything absurd in this policy of keeping people unemployed, with compensation, while at the same time offering them unpaid work.[300]

The fact that the unemployed still can manage economically at a minimum level — in the long run, the perspective for most of them is bleak, there are few chances of ever finding a regular job and benefits are bound to decline — is certainly one of the reasons for the fatalism characterizing Dutch public discussion about unemployment. Another reason — a cause as well as an effect of fatalism — is the prevailing notion that the only real solution to mass unemployment is reduction in working-time paid for by the workers through wage cuts. This is the prevailing wisdom in the Netherlands among all those who do not believe in the 'new industrial elan' — progressive Christian Democrats, most of the Social Democrats, the fragmented left-wing parties, and the trade unions. Among the largest of the trade unions, the FNV, however, enthusiasm is mellowing after the poor results of a policy involving endorsement of the necessity of higher profits in return for a non-committal promise that reduced working-time should be used for more employment.[301] Since then, unemployment has increased in the Netherlands by roughly the same amount as the total unemployment in Japan in 1984!

Working-time reduction is a historic goal of the labour movement, around which the May Day tradition of demonstrations
developed, and it was central to Marx's perspective of a classless
Communist society. But at that time the demand had a class-
struggle-based purpose in the fight for a society of freedom and
equality. Today, struggle in itself has little value. Much current
discussion of a shorter working week has lost contact with the classical tradition, to which many currents are even explicitly hostile
today. The effects of such an attitude can be learnt from the Dutch
experience.

The Dutch current government and the Dutch employers are
against a general reduction of working-time as a systematic policy;
the former are against legislation, the latter against binding general
collective agreements. Without struggle, there will be no major
reduction in working-time. But the progressive forces have largely
disarmed themselves already. They have done so by neglecting the
causes of mass unemployment in the Netherlands and by
neglecting the wide range of employment policy options available.
By concentrating their fire exclusively on shorter hours, the opposition has left current government policy out of range.

In fact, mass unemployment in the Netherlands is not a fatality
brought by the international crisis or by the contemporary stage of
economic development. Mass unemployment occurs in some
countries and not in others. The Dutch crisis is a consequence of
Dutch capitalism, of its political strength and of its economic
weakness. While little elan is displayed by most Dutch businessmen — a couple of multinationals apart[302] — their political
influence is staggering. Even in the United States, it would hardly
have been politically possible to have the main lines of government
policy explicitly laid down by the chairman of Exxon. Ronald
Reagan (on suitable occasions) takes pride in having a background
as a trade unionist (in the Actors' Guild); the current Dutch Premier is a former secretary of the Catholic employers' organization.

Dutch business has had a political chance which few, if any, of
its equivalents in other democratic capitalist countries have had.
Whether it has been successful in its own terms is of no concern
here. But for the majority of the population its policies have led to
a situation where only about half of the adult population has a job,
where unemployment is a mass phenomenon, and where the once
generous welfare state is being more and more cut into. In the
modest opinion of a foreign intellectual, the priority is not to re-

distribute the blows of Dutch capitalism, but to put a stop to the blows themselves.

Notes to Preface

1. Schmidt's first major effort was 'The Role of Parties in Shaping Macroeconomic Policy' in F. Castles ed., *The Impact of Parties*, London 1982. Also significant is his as yet unpublished paper, 'The Politics of Macroeconomic Policy'.
2. See however his monograph on Switzerland, *Der Schweizerische Weg zur Vollbeschäftigung*, Frankfurt 1985.
3. Cf. K. Armingeon, *Neo-korporatistische Einkommenspolitik*, Frankfurt 1983, p. 78.
4. F. Scharpf, *The Political Economy of Inflation and Unemployment in Western Europe*, Berlin 1981; 'Economic and Institutional Constraints of Full Employment Strategies: Sweden, Austria and West Germany (1973-1982)' in J. Goldthorpe ed. *Order and Conflict in Contemporary Capitalism*, Oxford 1984; 'Strategy Choice, Economic Feasibility and Institutional Constraints as Determinants of Full Employment Policies during the Recession' in K. Gerlach et al., eds., *Public Policy to Combat Unemployment in a Period of Economic Stagnation*, Frankfurt 1984.
5. J.E. Kolberg, P.A. Pettersen and K. Hagen, 'Arbeidsledighetens Komparative Politiske Økonomi', Fagbevegelsens Senter for Forskning og Dokumentasjon, Oslo 1983.
6. D. Aldcroft, *Full Employment: The Elusive Goal*, Brighton 1984.
7. Michael Bruno and Jeffrey Sachs, *The Economics of Worldwide Stagflation*, Oxford 1985.
8. P. Mosley, *The Making of Economic Policy*, Brighton 1984.

Notes to Summary and Conclusions

1. OECD, *Economic Outlook*, no. 36, December 1984, pp. 51, 177. The unemployment rate refers only to the fifteen of the twenty-four countries for which standardized rates of unemployment existed by December 1984. The twenty-four include all the major advanced countries except Denmark, Iceland, Luxemburg and Switzerland.
2. Ibid., p. 51.
3. The Economist Intelligence Unit. 'Europe 1990: A Challenge to Business', *Special Report*, no. 173, London 1984, p. 36.
4. EEC, *Analysis and Projection of Regional Documentation on Regional Policy in the Community*, Brussels 1984, pp. 54-8.
5. I am indebted here to the observations of the Swedish radio commentator Ann-Marie Boström.
6. Calculated from OECD, *Employment Outlook*, September 1984, p. 9; *Economic Outlook*, no. 36, p. 51.
7. From the beginning of 1985, the OECD, *Quarterly Labour Force Statistics* has started to publish standardized unemployment rates for Switzerland.

164

8. *Vrij Nederland*, 22 December 1984.

9. London 1984, p. 316.

10. W. Korpi, *The Democratic Class Struggle*, London 1983, esp. pp. 39ff.

11. A. Kjellberg, *Facklig Organisering i Tolv Länder*, Lund 1983, pp. 36-7; S. Mielke ed., *Internationales Gewekschaftshandbuch*, Opladen 1983.

12. M. Kalecki, 'Political Aspects of Full Employment', *Political Quarterly*, no. 1943.

13. P. McCracken et al., *Towards Full Employment and Price Stability*, Paris 1977.

14. Evaluation by the Swedish Central Bureau of Statistics for the Labour Market Board, reported in *Svenska Dagbladet*, 16 April 1984.

15. The *Times*, 11 June 1983.

16. *Handelsblatt*, 31 December 1984.

17. *Economic Outlook*, no. 36, pp. 51, 177.

18. Göran Therborn, 'The Prospects of Labour and the Transformation of Advanced Capitalism', *New Left Review*, no. 145, May-June 1984.

19. *Business Week*, 12 December 1984.

20. The *Economist*, 5 January 1985.

21. The very ambitious and interesting internationalist project for getting out of the crisis, which was launched and co-ordinated by Stuart Holland, came to nothing. See Stuart Holland ed., *Out of Crisis*, London 1982.

Notes to Part One: 'Grunemployment' and Paradoxical Economics of the Crisis

1. *Report of the Seventy-Fifth Annual Conference of the Labour Party*, London 1976, p. 189.

2. Centre for Policy Studies, *Conditions for Fuller Employment*, London 1978, p. 3.

3. Growth and inflation 1973-82: OECD, *Economic Outlook*, no. 36, December 1984, pp. 166, 175; growth and inflation 1984: OECD, *Main Economic Indicators*, March 1985, pp. 23, 186; unemployment: OECD, *Quarterly Labour Force Statistics*, no. 1, 1985, p. 76.

4. As above.

5. Denmark 1983: *Det Økonomiske Råd, Dansk Økonomi* (December 1983), Copenhagen 1983, p. 52; Denmark 1984; OECD, *Economic Outlook* no. 36, p. 51; all others: *Quarterly Labour Force Statistics* no. 1, 1985, p. 76. Even as I develop these analyses, new statistics are being published. Most of the discussion below will therefore use 1983 as a base year, the latest one for which figures are available. The 1983 figures are those given by the OECD in early 1985, in some cases they differ from those of the December 1984 *Economic Outlook*: Australia 9.8; Austria 4.2; Belgium 14.7; France 8.1; Germany 7.5; Italy 9.7. These changes do not affect the results of the statistical analysis.

6. *Economic Outlook* no. 38, pp. 171, 183; Danish unemployment from *Arbejdsloshedens Omkostninger i Norden*, Stockholm 1985, p. 17 and no. 38, p. 29. Labour force from OECD *Labour Force Statistics 1963-1983*, Paris 1985, p. 21 and *Employment Outlook*, Sept. 1985, p. 125.

7. *Quarterly Labour Force Statistics*, no. 1, 1985, p. 76: *Economic Outlook*

no. 36, p. 177. Danish data from G. Esping Andersen, *Politics Against Markets*, Princeton 1985, p. 240n. Andersen's is a very important work on Scandinavian Social Democracy, which unfortunately appeared too late for consideration here.

8. OECD, *National Accounts 1960-83*, pp. 83-106.

9. See note 6.

10. See note 8.

11. *Economic Outlook* no. 38, p. 172, 181, 183. For Danish unemployment, see note 6.

12. See note 11.

13. Trade: European Management Forum, *Report on International Competitiveness*, Geneva 1984, p. 148; oil imports: OECD, *Economic Outlook*, no. 33, p. 136 and OECD, *Economic Surveys: United Kingdom*, Paris 1984.

14. Export volume development calculated from OECD, *National Accounts 1960-1983*, p. 119.

15. OECD, *Employment Outlook*, September 1984, pp. 18 and 40.

16. The resilience of employment levels in the food industry during the crisis may turn out to have been a temporary break in a historical trend of decline. OECD, *Industry in Transition*, Paris 1983, p. 117.

17. Belgian, Dutch and Danish growth figures are calculated from comparisons of service employment in 1982, drawn from the *OECD Observer*, no. 127 and the *Eurostat Review 1971-1980*, Luxemburg 1982, p. 121. Other growth figures are from *Employment Outlook*, September 1983, p. 21. Service-sector size in 1974 from OECD, *Historical Statistics 1960-1980*, Paris 1982, p. 35.

18. Belgian and Italian industrial structures: Eurostat, *Employment and Unemployment 1974-1982*, Luxemburg 1983. Belgian production: *Economisch Zakboekje*, Antwerp 1983. British and Italian manufacturing employment in 1975: F. Blackaby ed., *De-industrialization*, London 1978, p. 237. Dutch manufacturing employment in 1975: *Tachtig Jaren Statistiek in Tijdreeksen 1899-1979*, The Hague 1979, p. 68. Australian manufacturing size and development: OECD, *Economic Surveys 1982-1983, Australia*, Paris 1983, pp. 39 and 71. Size of manufacturing employment and industrial structure for other countries: OECD, *Indicators of Industrial Activity*, 1984:1, Paris 1984, pp. 22-24.

19. OECD, *Industrial Robots*, Paris 1983, p. 51.

20. Data from table 3 and *Economic Outlook*, no. 35, p. 133.

21. Ibid., p. 133.

22. Labour costs: *Report on International Industrial Competitiveness*, p. 59. Employment: calculations from OECD, *Belgium Luxembourg*, Paris 1984, p. 34; OECD, *Finland*, Paris 1983, p. 55; OECD, *Main Economic Indicators 1964-1983*, Paris 1984, pp. 142, 243 and 425; OECD, *Indicators of Industrial Activity 1984*.

23. *Economic Outlook*, no. 35, p. 45.

24. Netherlands, *Nationale Rekeningen 1982*, The Hague 1983, pp. 75-6. All other countries: *Economic Outlook*, no.36, p. 63.

25. *Economic Outlook*, no. 36, p. 64.

26. Taxation (current government receipts): *Economic Outlook*, no. 35, p. 160. Social expenditure calculated from OECD, *Social Expenditure 1960-1990*, Paris 1985, pp. 79ff.

27. UN, *Economic Bulletin for Europe*, vol. 35, no. 4, September 1983, p. 292.

28. OECD, *High Unemployment – A Challenge for Income Support Policies*, Paris 1984, pp. 28, 197, 249; OECD, *Labour Force Statistics 1962-1982*, Paris 1984, p. 99.

29. *Arbejdsloshedens Omkostninger i Norden*, Stockholm 1983, p. 15, Ibid.

166

(1984), pp. 32, 52-3, 62; Statistiska Centralbyrån, *Ardetsmarknaden 1970-1983*, Stockholm 1984, pp. 124 and 133.

Notes to Part Two: Profiles of Unemployment

1. OECD, *Employment Outlook*, Paris, September 1984.
2. Ibid., p. 15.
3. Central to the ideological/political controversy is André Gorz, *Farewell to the Working Class*, London 1983. A major discussion was staged at the German Sociological Congress in 1982, published as *Krise der Arbeitsgesellschaft*, Frankfurt 1983. Another interesting contribution is Claus Offe, '*Arbeitsgesellschaft'*: *Strukturprobleme und Zukunftsperspectiven*, Frankfurt 1984.
4. A. Maddison, *Ontwikkelingsfasen van Het Kapitalisme*, Antwerp 1982, pp. 261-2; OECD, *Historical Statistics 1960-1980*, p. 36.
5. C. Sorrentino, 'International Comparisons of Labour Force Participation, 1960-1981', *Monthly Labour Review*, vol. 106, no. 2, February 1983, p. 30.
6. *Employment Outlook*, September 1984, p. 106.
7. Ibid., pp. 104-6.
8. G. Bruche and B. Casey, 'Arbeitsmarktspolitik und Stagflations-bedingungen', *Mitteilungen aus der Arbeitsmarkts- und Berufsforschung*, no. 3, 1982, p. 245.
9. *Sociaal-Economische Maandsstatistiek*, supplement, August 1984, p. 7.
10. *Arbetsmarknadspolitik under Ompṙovning*, SOU 1984:31, Stockholm 1984.
11. *Die Zeit*, no. 27, 1984, p. 24. It should be noted that actual overtime is not included in any of these figures; OECD, *Shorter Working Time*, Paris 1984, p. 33.
12. *Employment Outlook*, September 1984, pp. 27, 107.
13. *Labour Force Statistics 1963-1983*, Paris 1985, p. 25, and *Employment Outlook*, September 1985, p. 122.
14. Ibid., p. 45.
15. *Employment Outlook*, September 1984, pp. 33-4.
16. OECD, *The Challenge of Unemployment*, September 1984, p. 106.
17. *De Standaard*, 4 October 1984.
18. Employment Outlook, September 1984, p. 106.
19. *Monthly Labour Review*, March 1985, p. 62.
20. This summary is based on the text and tables together with material from United Nations, *Economic Bulletin for Europe*, vol. 35, no. 3, September 1983, pp. 292-3; OECD, *Labour Force Statistics 1962-1982*, part 3, Paris 1984 (which in spite of its title also provides data for 1983); OECD, *High Unemployment: A Challenge for Income Support Policies*, Paris 1984, pp. 29, 137, 244, 249; *Arbejdsløshedens Omkostninger i Norden; Arbetsmarknaden 1970-1983*, Stockholm 1984, pp. 124, 133, 150-5.
21. Central Statistical Office, *Social Trends 13*, London 1983, p. 19.
22. *Annuario Statistico Italiano*, Rome 1983, p. 12.
23. *Statistical Yearbook of Finland*, Helsinki 1983, p. 57.
24. *Statistisk Årbog 1983*, Copenhagen 1983, p. 29; *Statisk Årbok 1983*, Oslo 1983, pp.30, 33.
25. *Eurostat Review 1971-1980*, Luxemburg 1982, pp. 103, 108.
26. *Yearbook Australia 1982*, Canberra 1982, p. 139.

27. Calculations from OECD, *The Challenge of Unemployment*, Paris 1982, p. 126.

28. *Canada Yearbook 1980-81*, Ottawa 1981, p. 258.

29. *Statistical Abstract of the United States, 1982-83*, Washington DC 1982, p. 37.

30. *Yearbook Australia 1982*, p. 113.

31. *Canada Yearbook 1980-81*, pp. 130-59, OECD, *Economic Surveys: Canada*, Paris 1983, p. 5. In 1977-82 immigration accounted for 37 per cent of population growth, compared to 34.4 per cent in 1971-76 and 29.8 per cent in 1966-71.

32. *Statistical Abstract of the United States*, p. 86.

33. OECD, *Labour Force Statistics 1969-1980*, Paris 1982; OECD, *Employment Outlook*, Paris 1985.

34. OECD, *Historical Statistics 1960-1980*, Paris 1982, p. 24.

35. Ibid., and *Employment Outlook*, September 1984, p. 18.

36. *Historical Statistics 1960-1980*, p. 26.

37. OECD, *Indicators of Industrial Activity*, no. 2, 1984.

38. *Employment Outlook*, September 1984, pp. 40, 46; *Indicators of Industrial Activity*, no. 2, 1984.

39. *Employment Outlook*, September 1984, p. 47.

40. Calculations based on tables 3 and 17.

41. Swedish Employers Confederation, *Wages and Total Labour Costs for Workers: International Survey 1972-1982*, Stockholm, 1984, pp. 20, 74.

Notes to Part Three: Politics, Policies, Pressures and Constraints

1. The important attempts by Manfred Schmidt to provide a political explanation for variations in unemployment have centred on the second kind of politics. His latest formulation is to be found in an as yet unpublished paper, 'The Politics of Macroeconomic Policy'. A somewhat earlier formulation in English is his 'The Welfare State and the Economy in Periods of Economic Crisis: A Comparative Analysis of Twenty-Three OECD Nations, *European Journal of Political Research*, vol. 2, 1984. A pioneering contribution to the politics of full employment is Nixon Apple's 'The Rise and Fall of Full Employment Capitalism', *Studies in Political Economy*, no. 4, Autumn 1980.

2. Scharpf's most elaborate formulations to date may be found in his 'Strategy Choice, Economic Feasibility and Institutional Constraints as Determinants of Full Employment Policy during the Recession' in K. Gerlach et al., eds., *Public Policies to Combat Unemployment in a Period of Economic Stagnation*, Frankfurt 1984, pp. 67-114.

3. See D. Aldcroft, *Full Employment: The Elusive Goal*, Brighton 1984 and Philip Armstrong, Andrew Glyn and John Harrison, *Capitalism since World War II*, London 1984.

4. See B. Rothstein, 'The Success and Export of Swedish Labour Market Policy: The Organizational Connection to Policy', as yet unpublished.

5. F. Scharpf et al., eds., *Aktive Arbeitsmarktpolitik*, Frankfurt 1984; F. Scharpf and M. Brockmann eds., *Institutionelle Bedingungen der Arbeitsmarkt – und Beschäftigungspolitik*, Frankfurt 1985. Scharpf himself pays more attention to

incomes policy than to labour market policy.

6. For example, Jeremy Richardson and Roger Henning, *Unemployment*, Beverly Hills 1984, is a telling illustration of this. It is also a mine of information.

7. Unemployment figures for 1967-81 are taken from OECD *Economic Outlook*, no. 33, p. 169. Figures for 1982-83 come from *Economic Outlook*, no. 36, December 1984, p. 177. Danish figures derive from Richardson and Henning, p. 220 and from *Det Okonomiske Rad*, p. 52.

8. OECD, *Quarterly Labour Force Statistics*, 1984: 1, p. 13; *Economic Outlook*, no. 36, p. 177.

9. Bourgeois governments, in accordance not only with Marxist terminology but also with standard Swedish political parlance, are governments to the right of Social Democracy. Coalitions are combinations of bourgeois and workers' parties, distinguished by me according to the complexion of the dominant partner. Sources used here are K. van Beyme, *Parteien in Westlichen Demokratien*, Munich 1982, together with press reports from 1982.

10. Schmitter's basic texts may be found in Philippe Schmitter and Gerhard Lehmbruch eds., *Towards Corporatist Interest Intermediation*, Beverly Hills 1979.

11. Philippe Schmitter, 'Interest Intermediation and Regime Governability' in S. Berger ed., *Organizing Interests in Western Europe*, Cambridge 1981, p. 294.

12. G. Lehmbruch, 'Concentration and the Structure of Corporatist Networks' in J. Goldthorpe ed., *Order and Conflict in Contemporary Capitalism*, Oxford 1984.

13. K. Armingeon, *Neokorporatistische Einkommenspolitik*, Frankfurt 1983, p. 78. The countries covered were Belgium, Denmark, Finland, Ireland, Netherlands, Norway, Sweden and the UK. The most comprehensive study of European incomes policies is the massive work by R. Flanagan, D. Soskice and L. Ulman, *Unionism, Economic Stabilization and Incomes Policies*, Washington DC 1983. However, it is not written from a corporatist vantage point and it is not possible to characterize the work in a straightforward corporatist way.

14. Armingeon, p. 78. The countries covered were Belgium, Denmark, Finland, Ireland, Netherlands, Norway, Sweden and the UK.

15. R. Czada, 'Zwischen Arbeitsplatzinteresse und Modernisierungszwang' in H. Wimmer ed., *Wirtschafts- und Socialpartnerschaft in Osterreich*, Vienna 1984, pp. 161-2.

16. M. Schmidt, *Wohlfahrtsstaatliche Politik unter bürgerlichen und social-demokratischen Regierungen*, Frankfurt 1982, p. 126.

17. Ibid., p. 182.

18. M. Shaley, 'Strikes and the Crisis: Industrial Conflict and Unemployment in the Western Nations', *Economic and Industrial Democracy*, vol. 4, no. 4, November 1983, pp. 440 ff. Shaley's measure seems most appropriate here, the proportion of workers involved in industrial conflict (rather than days 'lost', a measure that can be inflated by a few prolonged conflicts in quite specific sectors) averaged by goemetrical means, thereby reducing the impact of exceptional years.

19. K. Eriksen and G. Lundestad eds., *Norsk Innenrikspolitik. Kilder til Moderne Historie II*, Oslo 1972, pp. 28 ff.

20. P.J. Bjerve, *Planning in Norway 1947-1956*, Amsterdam 1959.

21. O. Aukrust, *Norges Økonomi Efter Krigen*, Oslo 1965, pp. 112n, 367n.

22. G. Junne, 'Der Strukturpolitische Wettlauf Zwischen den Kapitalistischen Industrieländern', *Politische Vierteljahresschrift*, vol. 25, 1984, p. 137.

23. *Arbetarrörelsens Efterkrigsprogram*, Stockholm 1944.

24. B. Sodersten, 'Bostadspolitik och Bostadsforsorjning under Efter-kirgstiden' in B. Sodersten ed. *Svensk Ekonomi*, Stockholm 1970, p. 201.

25. The political conflicts around unemployment policy in 1932-33 centred around the wage level in public works and the size of the works. They were not about deflation versus reflation, nor were they about general budgetary principles, nor about whether the state should do something active to combat unemployment, cf. Göran Therborn, 'The Coming of Swedish Social Democracy' in *Instituto Feltrinelli, Annali 1984*, Milan 1984.

26. G. Rehn, 'Finansminisrarna, LO-ekonomerna och Arbetsmarknads-politiken' in *Ekonomisk Debatt och Ekonomisk Politik*, Nationalekonomiska Foreningen 100 ar, Stockholm 1977.

27. OECD, *Review of Manpower Policy in Denmark*, Paris 1974, p. 53. Figures do not include programmes specifically targeted for industrially depressed areas. If they were included, Sweden would head the list by 1.4 per cent, followed by Canada with 1.1 per cent and the UK with 0.9 per cent.

28. UN Economic Commission for Europe, *Economic Survey of Europe in 1949*, Geneva 1951, p. 63.

29. Ibid., p. 62.

30. E. Tuchfeldt, 'Die Schweizerische Arbeitsmarktsentwicklung — Ein Sonderfall?' in O. Issing ed., *Aktuelle Probleme der Arbeitslosigkeit*, Berlin 1978, p. 177.

31. R. Senti, 'Die Staatliche Wirtschaftspolitik' in E. Gruner ed., *Die Schweiz seit, 1945*, Berne 1972, pp. 102-6.

32. Tuchfeldt, p. 181.

33. Senti, p. 108 ff.

34. W. Beveridge, *Social Insurance and Other Services*, London 1942.

35. A. Deacon, 'Unemployment and Politics in Britain since 1945', in B. Showler and A. Sinfield eds., *The Workless State*, Oxford 1981, pp. 63-4.

36. A. Shonfield, *Modern Capitalism*, Oxford 1965, p. 94.

37. N. Apple, 'The Rise and Fall of Full Employment Capitalism', *Studies in Political Economy*, no. 4, 1980, p. 12.

38. B. Hansen, *Fiscal Policies in Seven Countries*, Paris 1969, p. 69. The evaluation of the good resources of budgetary policy in Britain is also taken from this source.

39. Ibid., p. 444.

40. Ibid., pp. 418-19.

41. P. Calvocoressi, *The British Experience 1945-75*, Harmondsworth 1979, p. 96. The increase in unemployment in Britain had no parallel at the time. Cf A. Maddison, *Ontiwikkelingsfasen van het Kapitalisme*, Utrecht-Antwerp 1982, p. 276.

42. Maddison, p. 276; Deacon, pp. 55-8.

43. Harold Wilson, *The Labour Government 1964-1970*, London 1971, pp. 447, 453, 456.

44. Richard Crossman, *The Diaries of a Cabinet Minister*, vol. 2, London 1976, p. 309.

45. Göran Therborn, 'Britain Left Out', *New Socialist*, no. 17, 1984.

46. Maddison, pp. 276, 318.

47. OECD, *Integrated Social Policy: A Review of the Austrian Experience*, Paris 1981, p. 41.

48. Maddison, p. 276.

170

49. H. Abele, 'Anmerkungen zur Wirtschaftgeschichte der Gegenwart: Österreich seit 1945', in H. Abele et al., eds., *Handbuch der Österreichischen Wirtschaftspolitik*, Vienna 1984, p. 15.

50. OECD, *Economic Surveys, Austria*, Paris 1982, p. 23.

51. CEEP, *Die Öffentliche Wirtschaft der Europaischen Gemeinschaft*, Berlin 1981, p. 154.

52. B. Marin, *Die Pariätische Kommission: Aufgeklärter Teknokorporatismus in Österreich*, Vienna 1982.

53. 58 and 38 per cent of employees respectively, A. Kjellberg, *Facklig organisering i tolv länder*, Lund 1983, pp. 76-7.

54. H. Andics, *Die Insel der Seligen*, Vienna 1980, pp. 341 ff; A. Pelinka, 'Austria's Political System' in OECD, *Integrated Social Policy*; G. Aichholzer, 'Arbeitsmarkt in Österreich', *Österreichische Zeitschrift fur Soziologie*, vol. 7, nos 3-4, 1982, pp. 69 ff.

55. E. Marz, 'Stagnation und Expansion', *Wirtschaft und Gesellschaft*, vol. 8, pp. 333 ff; F. Scharpf 'Economic and Institutional Constraints of Full Employment Strategies', *IIM/LMP* 83-20, Berlin 1983, p. 30.

56. Charles Johnson, MITI *and the Japanese Miracle*, Stanford 1984, p. 107.

57. Johnson, p. 216.

58. A. Shonfield, *In Defence of the Mixed Economy*, Oxford 1984, p. 107.

59. Maddison, p. 276.

60. Shonfield, *In Defence of the Mixed Economy*, p. 91; Johnson; C.G. Allen, *Japan's Economic Policy*, London; K. Sato ed., *Industry and Business in Japan*, pp. 104-5.

61. OECD, *Manpower Policy in Japan*, Paris 1973, pp. 104-5.

62. Apple, pp. 13-18.

63. B. Hansen, *Fiscal Policies in Seven Countries 1955-1965*, pp. 487-8.

64. P. Auer, 'Strategien der Arbeitsbeschaffung in Drei Ländern', *IIM/LMP 83-22*, Berlin 1983, pp. 31-2.

65. That is the conclusion that must be drawn from the overview of crisis policies in the OECD survey, *Australia*, Paris 1983.

66. Maddison, p. 275; Shonfield, *Modern Capitalism*, p. 85.

67. S. Nordengren, *Economic and Social Targets for Postwar France*, Lund 1972, p. 111.

68. Shonfield, *Modern Capitalism*, p. 272.

69. Ibid., p. 284.

70. K. Hennings, 'West Germany' in A. Boltho ed., *The European Economy*, London 1982, p. 490. The conclusion is mine.

71. Ibid., p. 475.

72. UN Economic Commission for Europe, p. 71.

73. Maddison, p. 276-7.

74. The tripartite and bipartite agreements and declarations in Belgium for the 1936-74 period are assembled in *Het Sociaal Overleg op Interprofessioneel Vlak*, Brussels 1974.

75. A good overview of early Finnish manpower policy is given in P. Kuusi, *Social Policy for the Sixties*, Helsinki 1964.

76. J.O. Andersson et al., 'Inkomstpolitiken i Finland' in *Inntektspolitikk i Norden 1945-80*, Finland, pp. 67-8.

77. OECD, *Manpower Policy in Finland*, Paris 1977, pp. 63 ff.

78. *Statistical Yearbook of Finland 1982*, Helsinki 1983, p. 80.

79. Nordiska Rådet/Nordiska Ministerrådet, *Rapport om Forslag Till Nordisk Handlingsplan för Ekonomisk Utvekling och Full Sysselsättning*, Stockholm 1983, p. 99.

80. Statistiska Centralbyran, *Arbetsmarknaden 1970-1983*, Stockholm 1984, p. 156.

81. Cf. C. Friisberg, *Den Nordiske Velfaerdstat*, Copenhagen 1982, pp. 16 ff; O. Bertolt et al., eds., *En Bygning vi Rejser*, vol. 3, Copenhagen, p. 171.

82. Maddison, p. 276.

83. G. Epsing-Andersen, *Social Class, Social Democracy and State Policy*, Copenhagen 1980, pp. 359 ff.

84. OECD, *Manpower Policy in Denmark*, Paris 1984.

85. On this aspect of the postwar settlement in Denmark, see further, P.E. de Hen, *Actieve en Re-Actieve Industriepolitiek in Nederland*, Amsterdam 1980; H. de Liagre Böhl et al., *Nederland Industrialiseert*, Nijmegen, parts one and two.

86. An example of this was the intervention of the Christian Democrat Prime Minister Van Agt in the parliamentary discussion of the 1981 budget. According to him, the Social Democrats' concern with everybody's right to a job is not only unrealistic, but also an expression of contempt for unpaid voluntary work (i.e., Christian charity). *Handelingen der Staten Generaal Tweede Kamer Zitting 1980-81*, p. 200.

87. F. de Jong Edz, *Om de Plaata ven de Arbeid*, Amsterdam 1956, pp. 206-7 (emphasis added).

88. W. Dercksen et al., eds., *Vijfendertig Jaar Ser-Adviezen*, vol. 1, Deventer 1982, pp. 481-2.

89. Calculated from W.S.P. Fortuyn, *Kerncijfers 1945-53*, Deventer 1983, pp. 83, 156.

90. SER, *Interimadvies Over de Aanvullende Werkgelegendheid*, Uitgaven 1967, p. 8. The principle was established in Sweden in 1933.

91. Ibid., pp. 3, 6.

92. SER, *Advies Over het Arbeidsmarktsbeleid*, 1969, pp. 8-9.

93. OECD, *Integrated Social Policy*, p. 27.

94. Calculations from R. Price and P. Muller, 'Structural Budget Indicators and the Interpretation of Fiscal Policy Stance in OECD Economies', *OECD Economic Studies*, no. 3, January 1984, p. 36. Switzerland was not included.

95. Since labour force developments in 1974 and 1975 in some countries were crucially affected by deliberate policies, the 1972-73 figures have been chosen. It should be noted that the OECD also contains some countries not included in this analysis; Greece, Iceland, Ireland, Luxemburg, New Zealand, Portugal, Spain and Turkey: OECD, *Historical Statistics 1960-1980*, Paris 1982, p. 23.

96. OECD, *Employment Outlook*, September 1984, p. 20.

97. *Economic Outlook*, July 1984, p. 152.

98. Ibid.

99. The basis of such generalizations is, unless otherwise stated, the OECD economic surveys of member countries, mainly those published in 1982-84.

100. OECD, *Japan*, July 1983, table 1, p. 8.

101. Ibid., p. 51.

102. *Economic Outlook*, July 1984, p. 159.

103. Ibid., pp. 159-60.

104. Calculations from OECD, Japan, p. 77; *Nationale Rekeningen 1982*, The Hague 1983, p. 143.

172

105. *Nationale Rekeningen,* pp. 158, 160.
106. Ibid., p. 158.
107. Ibid., pp. 159 f.
108. Ibid.
109. Scharpf, 'Economic and Institutional Constraints ...' pp. 26f; 'Strategy Choice, Economic Feasibility ...', pp. 95 ff.
110. 'Economic and Institutional Constraints ...', p. 52.
111. OECD, *Historical Statistics 1960-1980,* p. 94.
112. OECD, *Austria,* pp. 26, 33f.
113. OECD, *Switzerland,* p. 19.
114. *Economic Outlook,* no. 35, p. 165.
115. For a general overview in English, see R. Henning, 'Industrial Policy or Employment Policy?' in Richardson and Henning eds., pp. 192 ff. More penetrating is J. Johanneson, 'On the Outcome of Swedish Labour Market Policy from the 1960s to 1981' *IIM/LMP 82-13,* Berlin 1982. More theoretical in approach is B. Hjern, 'Selective Labour Market policy and the Non-Existence of Stable Philips Curves', *IIM/LMP 82/14,* Berlin 1982. See also the article by one of the two main architects of the policy: R. Meidner, 'Sweden: Approaching the Limits of Active Labour Market Policy' in Gerlach et al., eds., pp. 247-65.
116. Johannesson, p. 38; cf. G. Schmid, 'Die Entwicklung der Arbeitsmarkts-politik in Schweden und in der Bundesrepublik' in Scharpf et al., eds., *AktiveAr-beitsmarktpolitik*; also SOU, *Arbetsmarknadspolitik under Omprövning,* Stockholm 1982. In the 1982-83 figures, taken from the latter source, the multiplier effects of the measures upon unemployment are not included.
117. *Arbetsmarknadspolitik ...* pp. 59.
118. Calculated from *Centraal Economisch Plan 1984,* The Hague 1984, pp. 118 and 358.
119. Calculations based on M. Schmidt ed., *Westliche Industriegesellschaften,* Munich 1983, p. 45; Tuchfeldt, p. 171; OECD, *Historical Statistics,* p. 23.
120. Tuchfeldt, p. 173.
121. G. Junne, p. 137. The data were originally brought together by the West German government on the basis of OECD statistics.
122. OECD, *Norway,* Paris 1983, pp. 31-2.
123. Nordiska Rådet/Nordiska Ministerrådet, p. 99.
124. Schmidt, *Westliche Industriegesellschaften,* p. 45; OECD, *Historical Statistics,* pp. 23 and 37.
125. Scharpf, 'Economic and Institutional Constraints ...', p. 47.
126. Calculations based on E. Nowotny, 'Verstaatlichte und Private Industrie in der Rezession – Gemeinsamkeit und Unterschiede', WISO, vol. 2, no. 3, 1979, p. 76; *Statistiches Jahrbuch ...* 1983, p. 133; OECD, *Austria,* Paris 1982, p. 13. According to the statistical yearbook data, Nowotny understates the development of total manufacturing employment, giving an index of 94 instead of 97 in 1977 (1973=100).
127. OECD, *Japan,* p. 14.
128. OECD, *Job Losses in Major Industries,* Paris 1983, pp. 15-17.
129. Ibid., pp. 19, 21, 33, 77-8, Mitsubishi, for instance, entered into laundries and fast food as part of a corporate employment policy: A. Shonfield, *In Defence of the Mixed Economy,* p. 110.
130. ILO, *Social Labour Bulletin,* no. 2, 1983, p. 173; no. 4, 1983, pp. 469-70.
131. Johnson, MITI ... pp. 298 ff.

132. *Economic Outlook*, no. 35, p. 164.
133. Ibid., p. 27.
134. OECD, *Switzerland*, April 1978, pp. 34-5; April 1982, p. 23; *Economic Outlook*, no. 35, p. 165; Historical Statistics, p. 98.
135. *Switzerland*, May 1983, pp. 37 ff.
136. *Switzerland*, April 1982, pp. 21 ff.
137. *Switzerland*, May 1983, pp. 35-7.
138. A. Cappelen, '*Noen Hovedtrek ved Norsk Økonomi Etter 2 Verdenskrig*' in *Innenspolitik i Norden 1945-80*, Copenhagen 1981, pp. 106-7.
139. OECD, *Norway*, February 1983, pp. 23ff.
140. OECD, *Sweden*, July 1983, pp. 22ff; *Economic Outlook*, no. 35, p. 27 and p. 1964.
141. The OECD surveyors of Sweden in 1984 were rather impressed. OECD, *Suède*, February 1984, pp. 50ff. The perspective and plans of the government may be studied in *Regeringens Budgetförslag 1984/85 Sammanfattning*, Stockholm 1984.
142. OECD, *Austria*, February 1982, pp. 37-8; *Economic Outlook*, p. 51.
143. *Historical Statistics*, p. 98. *Economic Outlook*, no. 35, pp. 127-8.
144. OECD, *Suède*, February 1982, p. 19.
145. OECD, *Austria*, February 1982, p. 33.
146. *Economic Outlook*, no. 35, p. 114; no. 36, p. 128.
147. OECD, *Employment Outlook*, September 1984, p. 33; *Economic Outlook*, no. 36, p. 128.
148. The first people to assert the independence of Swedish currency policy — by leaving the EMS in autumn 1977 — were the bourgeois government. At the time they were bitterly attacked by the Social Democrats. It is little wonder that any serious political historian who wishes to avoid becoming a complete cynic must have a sense of humour. See G. Bohman, *Maktskiftet*, Stockholm 1984, pp. 394-5.
149. A. van Doorn, in *Elseviers Weekblad*, 19 September 1981.
150. The *Guardian*, 7 December 1984, p. 7.
151. *Time*, 19 November 1984, p. 20.
152. *Historical Statistics*, p. 37; *The Times*, 8 December 1984, p. 21.
153. *Economic Outlook*, no. 35, p. 157.
154. Ibid., p. 78.
155. OECD, *Denmark*, May 1983, p. 11n.
156. Det Økonomiska Råd, *Dansk Økonomi*, Copenhagen 1983, p. 28.
157. Ibid., p. 78.
158. Ibid., p. 52; *Historical Statistics*, p. 23; *Employment Outlook*, September 1983, p. 20.
159. *Historical Statistics*, p. 37.
160. OECD, *Denmark*, May 1983, p. 9; *Economic Outlook*, July 1984, p. 163.
161. *Dansk Økonomi*, p. 67.
162. I am here indebted to my friend Gunnar Olofsson of the Sociological Institute of Copenhagen University for his helpful observations.
163. *Historical Statistics*, p. 49.
164. *Dansk Økonomi*, pp. 52, 67, 72.
165. Ibid., pp. 70, 72; OECD, *Denmark*, p. 9.
166. *Denmark*, pp. 16-17.
167. Ibid., p. 60. I have also made calculations based on Danish labour-force statistics.

174

168. *Economic Outlook*, no. 35, p. 165.

169. Nordiska Arbetmarknadsutskottet, *Den Offentlige Sektorns Syssel-sättningsutveckling i Norden under 1970-talet*, Oslo 1983, p. 2.

170. *Arbetsmarknadsstatistisk Årsbok*, Stockholm 1983, p. 135.

171. *Denmark*, p. 9.

172. On *Denmark*, see P. Kampmann and J. Elm Larsen, *Dagpengereformen*, Copenhagen 1984; for the EEC as a whole see European Commission, *Comparative Overview of the Systems of Social Security*, Brussels 1982.

173. Kampmann and Larsen, p. 37.

174. Kampmann and Larsen, p. 43; Danish labour force statistics.

175. A. Sauvy, *Histoire Economique de la France entre les Deux Guerres*, Paris 1965.

176. I base this conclusion on my own experience of the Mitterrand election campaign. See also, *Le Monde Dossiers et Documents: L'Election Presidentielle 26 Avril*, Paris 1981.

177. Göran Therborn, 'The Prospects of Labour and the Transformation of Advanced Capitalism', *New Left Review*, 145, May-June 1984, pp. 16-17.

178. OECD, *France*, July 1984, pp. 19 and 25. This gives the consumer price index, which I have used to calculate the real value of transfers received.

179. Ibid., p. 26.

180. These are the terms in which the French experience is discussed by George Ross and Jane Jenson in their article, 'French Socialism in Crisis', in *Studies in Political Economy*, no. 11, Summer 1983. To my mind, this is the best short study in English of the early years of the Mitterrand regime.

181. An excellent basis for such an analysis is the brilliant book by Alain Lipietz, *L'Audace ou l'Enlisement*, Paris 1984.

182. *Economic Outlook*, no. 35, p. 164.

183. OECD, *France*, July 1984, p. 35; *Economic Outlook*, no. 35, p. 162.

184. OECD, *France*, p. 20.

185. Cf. Lipietz, pp. 198ff. Lipietz has argued that the franc was overvalued by 16 per cent in relation to the Deutschmark.

186. OECD, *France*, p. 12.

187. Ibid., p. 66.

188. Ross and Jensen, p. 91.

189. *Economic Outlook*, no. 35, p. 27.

190. Ibid., p. 29.

191. *Financial Times*, 13 September 1984.

192. French figure for 1980 from *Le Monde, Bilan Economique et Social 1983*, Paris 1984; 1981-83 figures from OECD, *France*, July 1984, p. 15; British figures from the *Financial Times*, 14 March 1984.

193. European Commission, *Analyse Comparative des Instrumens de la Politique de l'Emploi dans Certains Pays Membres*, Brussels and Luxemburg 1977, pp. 34ff.

194. G. Kuhlewind, 'Die Beschäftigungspolitik Frankreichs', *Mitteilungen aus der Arbeitsmarkts — und Berufsforschung*, no. 3, 1982, pp. 259-9; G. Bruche and B. Casey, 'Arbeitsmarktpolitik unter Stagflationsbedingung', in *Mitteilungen aus der Arbeitsmarkts — unde Berufsforschung*, no. 3, pp. 240-242.

195. Calculated from Kuhlewind, p. 295.

196. OECD, *France*, July 1984, pp. 26-7.

197. Calculated from J. Ralite, 'L'Efficacité des Aides Publiques pour

l'Emploi', *Economie et Politique*, Juillet-Août 1984, p. 23; OECD, *France*, pp. 26 and 69.

198. OECD, *Economic Outlook*, no. 35, pp. 152, 1673.

199. Ibid., p. 156.

200. *Historical Statistics*, p. 23.

201. Scharpf, 'Economic and Institutional Constraints ...', p. 50.

202. Schmid, p. 56. According to Schmid, Swedish labour market measures covered 2.25 per cent of the labour force, as against 2.54 per cent by German policies. Swedish experts give a figure for Sweden of 2.1 per cent of the labour force: *Arbetsmarknadspolitik ...*, p. 71. The real effect on the reduction of unemployment was lower in West Germany than in Sweden, due to the limited efficiency of short-time and winter work subsidies: a reduction of unemployment by 1.6 per cent of the labour-force in Germany, compared to 2.5 per cent in Sweden in 1975. And this is despite the fact that 1975 was a year in which there were great efforts in the field of labour market policy in Germany, whereas for Sweden it was a year of relative relaxation. See Schmid, p. 58 and for a broad international comparison – Bruche and Casey, pp. 232-50.

203. The story is told by Scharpf: 'Economic and Institutional Constraints ...' pp. 28-33 and by K. Hennings, p. 494.

204. *Historical Statistics*, pp. 93-4.

205. *Economic Outlook*, no. 35, p. 154.

206. Ibid., p. 161.

207. Ibid., p. 154.

208. Hennings, pp. 494-5.

209. OECD, *Germany*, June 1984, pp. 29 and 57.

210. *Economic Outlook*, no. 35, p. 156; Germany, pp. 70-1.

211. D. Webber, 'Combating or Acquiescing in Unemployment? Crisis Management in Sweden and West Germany', *West European Politics*, vol. 6, no. 1, January 1983, pp. 24-5 and 40-1.

212. Calculated from Schmid, p. 51.

213. Not all the measures included by Schmid have been included in later assessments of German policy. As far as programmes of vocational training and job creation go: 168,000 people were employed in 1975 and 166,000 in 1982, in 1983 the figure was 183,000. Figures from: Autorengemeinschaft, 'Die Arbeitsmarkt in der Bundesrepublik Deutschland in den Jahren 1983 and 1984 — insgesamt und regional' in *Mitteilungen aus der Arbeitsmarkt- und Berufsforschung*, no. 4, 1983, p. 344.

214. Ibid.

215. 1984 figure from *Frankfurter Allgemeine Zeitung*, 11 October 1984.

216. *Economic Outlook*, no. 36, pp. 170, 177.

217. OECD, *Italy*, May 1984, p. 57.

218. *Economic Outlook*, no. 36, p. 61.

219. Ibid., pp. 63-4; *Employment Outlook*, September 1984, p. 40; *Italy*, May 1984, p. 52.

220. *Italy*, p. 27.

221. Ibid., p. 72; *Economic Outlook*, no. 36, p. 179; European Management Forum, *Report on International Industrial Competitiveness*, Geneva 1984, p. 59.

222. *Italy*, p. 42.

223. *Economic Outlook*, no. 36, p. 173.

224. *Italy*, p. 24.

176

225. Ibid., p. 36ff; *Economic Outlook*, no. 36, pp. 119ff.

226. *Employment Outlook*, September 1984, pp. 33-4.

227. Figure for January 1985, seasonally adjusted, from OECD, *Quarterly Labour Force Statistics*, 1985, no. 1, p. 84.

228. *Economic Outlook*, no. 36, p. 170.

229. For economists, the Thatcher record is, of course, not only a legitimate, but also an interesting object of study. What seems to be the best econometric account of the British jobs holocaust was provided by Richard Layard and Stephen Nickel in the first 1985 issue of the *National Economic Institute Review*. While the rise of unemployment in the 1970s could be relegated to a wide combination of econometric variables, 78 per cent of the explained increase between the 1975-79 and the 1980-83 periods could be put down to lack of demand.

230. OECD, *Belgium*, April 1982, p. 15.

231. *Economic Outlook*, July 1984, p. 165.

232. Ibid., p. 132; OECD, *Belgium, Luxembourg*, April 1982, pp. 34, 58.

233. *Economic Outlook*, July 1984, p. 161.

234. *De Standaard*, 21 October 1983.

235. *Belgium Luxembourg*, p. 39.

236. *European Management Forum*, p. 156.

237. *Belgium Luxembourg*, p. 31.

238. *Historical Statistics*, p. 94.

239. W. van Rijckeghem, 'Benelux', in Boltho ed., p. 604.

240. Calculated from S. Lambert, *L'Année Sociale 1980*, Brussels 1982, p. 216.

241. Calculated from *Economisch Zakboekje 1983*, no. 1, Antwerp 1983, p. 36 (excluding compensatory early retirement regulations); *Arbeidsblad*, vol. 83, nos. 4-5, April-May 1982, p. 314 (handicapped in special employment); *Belgium Luxembourg*, p. 70 (labour force base).

242. *Belgium Luxembourg*, pp. 20ff, 56ff.

243. Ibid., p. 42.

244. European Management Forum, p. 90.

245. *Belgium Luxembourg*, May 1983, p. 17.

246. Review of social security by the European Community (1982).

247. *Economic Outlook*, no. 36, p. 177.

248. Ibid., p. 166.

249. Ibid., p. 170.

250. *Historical Statistics*, p. 23.

251. *Employment Outlook*, September 1984, p. 20.

252. *Historical Statistics*, p. 36.

253. Dutch figures from *Fortuyn*, p. 243; comparative data from *Historical Statistics*, p. 24.

254. *Historical Statistics*, pp. 26-7.

255. Centraal Bureau voor de Statistiek, *Tachtig Jaren Statistiek in Tijdreeksen*, The Hague 1979, pp. 66, 185; *Sociale Mandstatistiek 1978*.

256. Rijckeghem, p. 603. Austrian and German figures from Scharpf, 'Economic and Institutional Constraints', p. 50.

257. Bruche and Casey, p. 237 and *Historical Statistics*, p. 32. But West German work programmes for the handicapped cover only 0.3 per cent of the labour force for 1980; figures from Schmid, p. 52.

258. Ibid., p. 237.

259. Dutch expenditure from L. Hoffman, 'Het Beleid van het Ministerie van

Sociale Zaken en Werkgelenheid' in A. van Duijn ed., *Overheidsbeleid en Werkgelenheid*, Deventer, 1984, p. 114; Swedish figures from Schmid, p. 49.

260. *Historical Statistics*, pp. 93-4.

261. This story is told by Duisenberg himself in W. Gortzak ed., *De Kleine Stappen van het Kabinet Den Uyl*, Deventer 1978, pp. 31ff. According to Duisenberg, his more restrictive view had already been adopted in essence after a discussion in the inner cabinet in January 1975.

262. N. van Rossum ed, *Sociaal Economisch Jaarboek 1975-1976*, Amsterdam 1975, p. 64.

263. *Economic Outlook*, no. 35, p. 160.

264. *Handeling der Staten Generaal: Ziting der Tweede Kamer 1974-75*, 13, 318 no. 1, p. 42.

265. Ibid., pp. 98-118. In an interview, C.A. van den Beld, the head of the Plan-bureau, put the message more bluntly, 'The best defence against structural unemployment is to cut the costs of private enterprise and above all to cut wage costs', Van Rossum, p. 64.

266. H. den Hartog and H.S. Tjan, 'Investeringen, Lonen, Prijzen en Arbeidsplaatsen', *Centraal Planbureau papers*, no. 8, The Hague 1974.

267. Cf P. Kramer, 'Twijfels rond de Afwenteling in het model Vintaf II', *Economisch-Statistische Berichten*, 21 November 1979, p. 1225.

268. *Historical Statistics*, pp. 26, 87.

269. This type of modelling preceded that of den Hartog and Tjan, and is exemplified by the 69C model presented in the Planbureau in the *Centraal Economisch Plan 1981*. A textbook exposition is given by T. van Klundert, *Loonen en Werkgelegenheid*, Leiden 1977. Such calculations are neither made, nor taken seriously, in any other country.

270. For a comparative characterization of Dutch postwar planning see Shonfield, *Modern Capitalism*, especially pp. 211-20.

271. See, for instance, the article by J.C. Wiebrand, 'Het Gaat nit om Slikken of Stikken, maar om Slikken en 'n beetje Stikken', *De Volkskrant*, 20 September 1984.

272. NRC *Handelsblad*, 18 September 1984.

273. *Economic Outlook*, no. 36, pp. 44. 166.

274. *Economic Outlook*, 1984, p. 20; 1983, p. 18.

275. *Economic Outlook*, no. 36, pp. 133-4, 177.

276. Calculated from *Sociale Maandstatistiek*, no. 3, 1984, p. 18 (Dutch labour force); *Arbetsmarknadsstatistisk Årsbok 1983*, p. 40 (Swedish labour force in 1979); *Arbetsmarknadspolitik under Omprovning*, p. 31; Economic Outlook, no. 35, p. 163 (unemployment rates).

277. Participation rates from *Employment Outlook*, September 1983, p. 86; Unemployment rates from *Economic Outlook*, no.35, p. 163. Dutch women, long excluded from the labour market, have increased their participation during the crisis by more than the OECD average. On the other hand, female participation has increased less in absolute terms than in Sweden (Sweden +2.4 per cent; Netherlands +2.3 per cent), *Employment Outlook*, 1983, p. 18.

278. *Economic Outlook*, no. 35, p. 156; OECD, *Netherlands*, February 1984, p. 18.

279. The first report, *Plaats en toekomst van de nederlandse industrie*, came out in late 1980 and was immediately given government support, *Tweede Kamer, zitting 1980-91*, 16513, no. 1. The other reports, together with some of the reaction to

178

them, are collected in H. van Dellen ed., *Een Nieuw Elan*, Deventer, 1984.

280. *Werkgelegenheidsnota 83-84, Tweede Kamer, vergaderjaar* 1983-84, 18102, nos. 1-2, pp. 6ff.

281. *Netherlands*, p. 34.

282. Ibid., p. 54.

283. *Handelingen der Staten Generaal 1980-81, Miljoenennota 1982*, p. 34.

284. *Werkgelenheidsnota* 83-84, p. 5.

285. Ministerie van Binnenlandse Zaken en Sociaal en Cultureel Planbureau, *Over Voorzieningsgebruik en Personeel in de Kwartaire Sector 1983-87*, The Hague 1983, p. 137.

286. *Handelingen* ... p. 200.

287. *Handelingen*, 1700, no. 1. For an overview of Dutch policy and discussion of the crisis in 1981, and for other suggestions, I am indebted to one of my students, Wessel Visser, who has written an MA thesis on the subject.

288. *Handelingen* ... p. 376.

289. *Handelingen* ... 17341,no. 4, p. 2.

290. Centraal Planbureau, *Centraal Economisch Plan 1984*, p. 97.

291. Calculations on the basis of Statistiska Centralbyrån, *Perspektiv pa Välfärden*, Stockholm 1982; p. 73; Central Statistical Office, *Social Trends 13*, London 1982, p. 65; UN, *Demographic Indicators of Countries*, New York 1982 (proportion of old people).

292. *Centraal Economisch Plan 1984*, p. 96.

293. Ministry of Social Affairs and Employment, *Financiele Nota Sociale Zekerheid 1985*, The Hague 1984.

294. Exchange rates on 31 December 1984 from OECD, *Main Economic Indicators*, February 1985, p. 189.

295. *Svenska Dagbladet*, 22 November 1984.

296. Ibid., 1 December 1984.

297. Ibid., 14 December 1984; De Volkskrant, 21 December 1984.

298. *Sociale Maandsstatistiek*, no. 8, 1984, p. 79 and no. 3, 1984, p. 18.

299. *Centraal Economisch Plan 1984*, p. 320.

300. The calculation has been made by the Association of Dutch Municipalities, *De Volkskrant*, 10 August 1984.

301. Wagner played an important role in bringing about this remarkable agreement, see H. van Dellen ed., pp. 326-7.

302. As far as having a 'forward-looking innovative orientation', Dutch businessmen have a rather mediocre record, ranking below even Sweden with its strong public sector. European Management Forum, p. 182.

INDEX

180 *Index*